Fenway

That comes back to why the ballparks matter to us — because exactly

comparable people played a comparable game in this ballpark for generation after generation.

— GEORGE F. WILL

Fenway

A BIOGRAPHY IN WORDS AND PICTURES

EXPANDED AND UPDATED

DAN SHAUGHNESSY

AND

STAN GROSSFELD

HOUGHTON MIFFLIN COMPANY

BOSTON   NEW YORK

2007

For the two Sams

For information about permission to reproduce selections from this book, write to Permissions, Houghton Mifflin Company, 215 Park Avenue South, New York, New York 10003.

Visit our Web site: www.houghtonmifflinbooks.com.

Library of Congress Cataloging-in-Publication Data
Shaughnessy, Dan.
    Fenway : a biography in words and pictures / Dan Shaughnessy and Stan Grossfeld ; [new foreword by Leigh Montville]. — Expanded and updated.
        p. cm.
    ISBN-13: 978-0-618-73736-9
    ISBN-10: 0-618-73736-7
    1. Fenway Park (Boston, Mass.) — History. 2. Fenway Park (Boston, Mass.) — History — Pictorial works. 3. Boston Red Sox (Baseball team) — History. I. Grossfeld, Stan. II. Title.
    GV416.B674S53 2007
    796.357'06874461 — dc22   2006035457

Printed in the United States of America

QWT 10 9 8 7 6 5 4 3 2 1

PHOTO CREDITS

Boston Globe: pp. 1, 49, 54–55, 59.
*Boston Globe/*Stan Grossfeld: pp. 176, 184–185.
Boston Red Sox: p. 15.
John F. Kennedy Library: p. 63.
Sports Museum of New England: pp. 32, 46, 50–51, 52, 57.
Leslie Jones, courtesy of Boston Public Library, Print Department: pp. 30–31, 34, 41, 44–45, 56, 60.

BOOK DESIGN

Bill Marr, Open Books, LLC, Edgewater, Maryland

When they raze Fenway,

it'll be like cutting down an old tree.

Count the rings. There's one for each celebration

and heartache suffered by Red Sox fans.

— DAN SHAUGHNESSY

21   FOREWORD TO THE REVISED EDITION   *by Leigh Montville*

28   FOREWORD   *by Ted Williams*

39   INTRODUCTION   *by Dan Shaughnessy*

45   **Historic Fenway**

65   **The "New" Old Fenway**

85   **Game Day**

137   **The Wall**

149   **2004: An Alternative Universe**

163   **Fenway Memories**

164   DAVID HALBERSTAM

166   STEPHEN KING

168   JAMES TAYLOR

169   DORIS KEARNS GOODWIN

170   YO-YO MA

171   JIM PALMER

172   BUD SELIG

173   TIM RUSSERT

174   JOHN HENRY

175   SENATOR EDWARD M. KENNEDY

176   BUCKY DENT

178   DENNIS ECKERSLEY

179   DON ZIMMER

181   JAMES EARL JONES

182   CARL YASTRZEMSKI

190   ACKNOWLEDGMENTS

FENWAY PARK

FENWAY

YAWKEY WAY

1903 1904 1912 1915

BOSTON

by Leigh Montville

I didn't like this book when it first came out in 1999. Oh, the writing by Dan Shaughnessy was terrific and Stan Grossfeld's pictures were nothing less than X-rays of the soul of a baseball summer in Boston, but I hated the plot. I hated the ending.

Fenway: A Biography in Words and Pictures. Ugh.

The sad truth about most biographies, except maybe the New Testament, is that they finish badly. The subject, the character under consideration, always lives a grand and eventful life of accomplishment and tumult, then falters in the final few chapters. An incurable disease arrives. A wrong turn is made on a snowy, fateful night. An assassin, oh my gosh, appears at the presidential box in Ford's Theatre. The credits in the movie that follows roll over a scene at a graveside service.

That was the case here. The fable had run out for the fabled old ballyard on Yawkey Way by the end of this book. Plans not only were afoot for a new baseball palace to be erected across the street, but a man could look at one of those HO-gauge models of what was to come. Here was where we would enter the fresh, new baseball environment. There was where we would order a gourmet Italian soybean sausage and an imported German lo-carb beer. Here was where we would sit in amphitheater comfort, fully enjoying the multimedia glories to come. The glories of the past, alas, were not part of the future presentation.

Shaughnessy and Grossfeld were mostly performing a public service. They had preserved the memories, pressed between the pages like a faded boutonniere from the high school prom. The book was destined to be a keepsake, probably stashed on a shelf next to the authentic original Fenway Park brick

that had been pulled from the rubble. Maybe in the same room with an authentic original Fenway grandstand seat. My God, how did people ever sit in those things?

"Look at this," an old-timer, OK, me, was supposed to say to his grandson as he turned the pages of *Fenway: A Biography in Words and Pictures.* "This was where Ted Williams played. Where Yaz played. Where Bucky Dent, excuse my language, hit that home run in 1978."

I hated the thought.

I was a Fenway preservationist. I wanted the real thing to keep standing for all the cornball, cliché reasons. Comfort for history was a fine deal to me. I wanted to walk where I walked with my father when I was nine years old, sit where I sat with Dickie Jones when we hitchhiked 100 miles to the city to see a twilight doubleheader in college. I'd been to this place about a billion times in almost forty years as a sportswriter. I wanted to hear the voices of departed friends and enemies whispering in the wind, typewriters still clacking in my mind. Personal, greedy, I wanted.

"Finish your cotton candy," I wanted to say during lessons on Fenway lore to my grandson. "Here comes the ice cream guy. And watch out for a foul ball."

Another thing wrong with the plot was that The Guy never got The Girl. Terrible. Unrequited love was the constant theme. Fenway was a civic monument to civic frustration. The cavalry never arrived to save the day. The Indians— certainly the ones from Cleveland in 1948—always won the battles in the end. The whole gooey, curse-filled business of the Red Sox never measuring up, never finishing the job and winning a World Series, was tied to the ballpark. Fenway was a burial ground for all grand expectations.

What kind of story was that?

If this were fiction, I would have called Shaughnessy and suggested a few changes. Then, again, he probably would have thought of them himself. The goal would have been to bring in a lot more bluebirds and a few genuine rainbows. It would have been hokey Hollywood stuff, of course, but isn't that what sells? Isn't that what we really want? Get the modern version of Jimmy Stewart. Take the last pages from the script for *It's a Wonderful Life*. Yeah, that's the ticket.

The words would flow. First off, we bring in some new owners. Make them a sketchy group of characters at first, out-of-towners, carpetbaggers, sure to make bad things even worse. Make them hem a little, haw a little more, wait a minute, make them reconsider the decisions that were already in place. Wait a minute. Is there a chance for alternative medicine? A chance for an alternative ending?

A Band-Aid here. A chiropractic adjustment there. A food court in a new concourse. Seats on top of the left field wall. (Is this really happening? Is this Fenway Park?) A designated hitter from Minnesota. A teen-aged general manager from just around the corner. A pitcher from that *Spirit of '76* painting in Marblehead, blood on his sock? A roll past the dastardly New York Yankees? A triumphant march to the World Series championship? A lineup of pastel-painted World War II ducks in the outfield to take the heroes on a Lindbergh parade through the ticker tape of downtown?

Think of every great fictional sports story you can, from *Hoosiers* to *Slapshot* to *Bull Durham* to *The Bad News Bears*. The plot is the same. The heroes are dead, gone, done. Hopeless. Somewhere in the closing pages, magic intercedes. Shaky hands become steady. Balls that bounced the wrong way now bounce true. Unlikely heroes emerge. Fans are in a fine dither. Headlines are bold. Everyone is singing "Sweet Caroline" at the end, the trophy on display at American Legion halls and fraternal lodges around the region.

"Dead?" some doctor proclaims over the patient. "This guy is going to live for a long, long time. He'll live longer than all the rest of us."

Eight years have passed since the first publication of *Fenway: A Biography in Words and Pictures*. I can't say enough for the editing job that real life has done for this book. The rest has been solid reporting. Shaughnessy and Grossfeld have gone back and chronicled all the changes with their usual talent and imagination. The grim tale has turned giddy.

Read this book.

Four stars (out of four). Can't help myself. I'm a sucker for a happy ending.

Winthrop, Massachusetts
October 2006

by Ted Williams

When I walked into Fenway Park for the first time in 1939, it certainly looked like a different kind of ballpark. I didn't know if it was good or bad. I knew the right field fence was quite a little ways away. I didn't think it was a hitters' park at all. Right field

was 25 feet longer then than it is now. Center field was always a nice target, which was a great thing for a hitter. Any time you have too short a park in center, you're going to run into a lot of runs and a lot of problems. I don't think I hit my first home run to left field until four years after the first time I played at Fenway. And I told the clubhouse boy I'd never hit another one. He said, "Oh, yes, you will." I never saw many balls hit that way by left-handed hitters who pulled the ball. Charlie Keller could hit them up there. But there weren't as many balls hit long into left field into the screen and now it seems a lot of guys do it. I think that's because of bigger and stronger guys and I think it's because of the ball.

There were no bullpens out there my rookie year, and they thought they had a pretty good young hitter in me. I guess they figured, "We can improve the park and not hurt him any." I think they thought too much of me and then I didn't hit as many home runs my second year. They were pitching me tougher and it was a little harder. Still, I hit .344. But certainly those bullpens were an advantage. They made the ballpark 20 feet shorter.

I played that big right field my first year, but they moved me to left right away. That's an easier part of the ballpark, and they did that for a lot of big hitters. The wall used to be a little different. It was not quite as high and there was a little more of a bank going up to the wall. If you played there all the time, you got accustomed to the ballpark a little bit. I practiced out there, but in those days, the wall partitions weren't as consistent—they were every four feet or so. You'd get a

Three days before his eightieth birthday, Ted Williams demonstrates his hitting technique at his kitchen table in Hernando, Florida.

dead spot and down the ball would go, or you'd get a live spot and it would come back. In some ways, it was a little tougher then because now they come off a little more uniform. I don't remember any balls coming off the ladder. I know we had some funny bounces. You'd go over to back the center fielder up and the damn ball would go into right field. When I played left field, I talked to the guy in the scoreboard. I wanted to know what was going on and what other guys around the league were doing.

I'm glad they're going to change Fenway. I think the park has hurt the game some. I've seen a lot of wonderfully pitched ball games there get screwed up because some little pop fly hits up against that fence. Any time you're helping the hitter or helping the pitcher too much, you're hurting the game. And the thing about this game is that it's been so well balanced with so few changes. Boy, they were lucky to come up with it just like they did.

You are awfully close to the fans at Fenway. I would rather be a little bit farther away from the fans, because when I played I could hear everything. I had rabbit ears. I know the fans like to get close to the field, and there's certain ways you can do it so it doesn't interfere with the game. The fans didn't seem too close when I was in the on-deck circle. All the people who were that close were loyal Red Sox fans. But when I'd go out toward left field I'd get guys out there who weren't so nice.

But center and left field at Fenway are the worst parts about that ballpark. It makes it a little unfair because the greatest advantage to a hitter is when you hit the ball to center. But that's not supposed to be the way it is. It should be the pulled ball that helps the hitter the most. But center and left field in Fenway make it easier because you can wait longer and slap at the ball, which a lot of guys do now, and they get a little cheap hit out there and it takes away from the game. It's only 379 feet to left center. That's kind of close.

Any time you strengthen the pitcher's position more than it should be, or the hitter's position more than it should be, it takes away from the game. Because it's such a balanced game. The pitcher's got to have a reasonable chance in a reasonable ballpark. And so does the hitter. If you don't, you're going to get a low-scoring game in the pitcher's ballpark and a lot of cheap hits in the hitter's ballpark.

Ted, 1939

A lot of guys complained about the background. I never did. I guess the worst situation is when a big left-hander's pitching and the right-handers are looking up into that light in right center. That bothered a lot of guys, but I was used to the ballpark. Plus, there wasn't much foul territory, and that was an advantage for the hitter. But they've enlarged that a little bit since I was there. And I think they tried to keep fans out of that triangle area in center for a while—if they didn't sell out.

I'll tell you what: baseball has not kept pace with some of the improvements that can be made in a ballpark as far as background is concerned. There are three or four new parks that hurt hitters because the backgrounds are bad. Baltimore, when it was first put in, had lights low, and the pitchers threw right out of the lights. And Chicago, when I first went in there, they had a little bitty background. But they've made a lot of improvements, and those are things that have to be improved in the new park in Boston.

But Fenway was like a home to me. It sure was. I was there as long and as often and as much as anybody that I ever knew. I used to go early and get out late. I came in early so I could have some peace and quiet, and if I had to do anything or check anything, I could do it easily. And a lot of mail was delivered to me there. I loved to talk to the trainer and get a lot of my questions answered. I left the park late because I wanted the crowd to disperse.

I can remember the clubhouse. We had little wire seats and little folding

chairs. It wasn't as big as it is now, but as long as I was there, they were always improving the park. But they couldn't improve it. Sure, they could make the seats a little better and make this and that a little better—a little bullpen out there—but basically the park has so many nooks and circles and deflections, and that makes it tough.

When I was at Fenway, there was no place under the stands to hit. When I came back to manage with the Senators, they had improved the visitors' clubhouse because it needed it the most.

When I played in Boston, I never sat at the far end of the dugout. I was always up close, next to the bat rack. I'd have six or eight bats in there and six or eight bats in my locker, and I would try one every now and then. If I thought it was good wood, I'd put it aside, and if anybody wanted a bat of mine, I'd give 'em one of the rejects.

They've been to the World Series in that ballpark. I always thought we had a lot of bad breaks there. When they tear it down, I think it will be a good thing, I really do. Some great pitchers couldn't win in that ballpark. So it'll be a great thing when it happens. Maybe I played so long and played so many games there that I've seen too many great performances get cut in the heart by a bloop hit someplace. Sometimes the configuration of the ballpark just made it unfair.

I love the fans in New England. They're the greatest. They've had some problem years, but they're still hanging in there. All I can tell you about Boston is that the fans cannot be beat. And I hope they win a World Series. I don't want to live to be a helluva lot older than I am, but I want to tell you something. Someday, I would like to look in the stars and say, "Damn, we did it."

Hernando, Florida
August 1998

We love baseball

because it seizes and retains the past,

Dan Shaughnessy, 1968

by Dan Shaughnessy

It's personal.

There's no other way to explain the sentimental feelings many of us have for old, inanimate objects like sweaters, cars, houses, and baseball parks. I still have the maroon wool cardigan that my coach, John Fahey, gave me in 1969 (the year Tony C.

staged his dramatic comeback) when I lettered in baseball as a sophomore at Groton High School. The sweater has a big "G" on the right side, and for more than two years I got to walk the corridors of GHS feeling cool. I haven't worn that sweater since the early '70s, but I could never throw it away.

Then there's the 1987 maroon Volvo DL station wagon that was in my driveway for sixteen years. We brought my youngest child, Sam, home from the hospital in that car on October 4, 1987 (the day Roger Clemens won his twentieth to clinch his second straight Cy Young trophy), and I'd hoped to see Sam drive the clunky wagon to his high school baseball games, but the old bucket of bolts gave out early in the new millennium.

The house in which I grew up was built early in the last century, and my folks owned it from 1946 (when the Red Sox played the Cardinals in the World Series) until my mom sold it in the spring of 1988 (the year of Joe Morgan Magic at Fenway). On the last night, three of my siblings, my mom, and I sat in folding chairs around a card table in the empty living room and ate Chinese take-out. We told growing-up stories for the last time in the drafty old Victorian, then said good-bye. It was teary, and I remember it as the only

time my brother ever hugged me. It's been more than ten years since that night, and my oldest sister, now in her sixties, drives past the house on a regular basis yet still cannot bear to look.

It's personal.

Cynics are having a field day with folks like myself. I think it all started with Donald Hall's wonderful "Fathers Playing Catch with Sons" (1985). The baseball-as-life metaphor has become a droopy cliché, and ever since Ken Burns carpet-bombed us with eighteen hours of baseball history and folklore in 1994—complete with endless head shots of literati waxing poetic on the sport—it has been fashionable to bash those who hold baseball close to their heart.

Someday Fenway will be gone, and if it happens in my lifetime, I plan to spend some time in the empty yard, remembering all the things that happened there and contemplating what it has meant to my life. When they raze Fenway, it'll be like cutting down an old tree. Count the rings. There's one for each celebration and heartache suffered by Red Sox fans.

Detroit fans said goodbye to Tiger Stadium in 1999, and much was lost when they shuttered the old ballyard at the corner of Michigan and Trumbull. They have a fancy new ballpark in downtown Detroit, but all those bells, whistles, and theme park components can't replace the history of old Tiger Stadium.

The Red Sox first started playing big league ball in Fenway on April 20, 1912, just a few days after the White Star liner *Titanic* sank to the bottom of the North Atlantic. The collective memory of Red Sox Nation no longer goes back to the days before Fenway. It stands as the only place any of us remember the Red Sox playing home games. And so many of those memories are merged with our own life passages.

More than any sport, baseball is about generations. Watching a baseball game, parents and kids have time to talk with one another. There is plenty of time between pitches and between innings. Meanwhile, the major league marketing czars haven't yet bombarded us with rock music between pitches (though it's probably coming), and this rare silence, coupled with the pace of the game, allows for conversation and even storytelling in the stands. This makes baseball unique. Try making conversation during a Magic–Lakers game amid the din of the O-Rena in downtown, yahoo Orlando.

Most of us, later in life, remember going to baseball games with Dad and Mom. And as parents, we cherish the first visits to Fenway with our own children. I've yet to meet a New England Patriots fan who remembers his first visit with Dad to Foxborough. Quite simply, none of the other three major sports offers family fun the way baseball does. The other games are too expensive, too loud, and—in the case of all football and some hockey games—too rowdy.

Apart from my childhood home and the one where I now live, Fenway Park is just about my favorite place on Earth. Some folks would name Disneyland, Walden Pond, Yellowstone, or a sweet summer spot on old Cape Cod. Good for them. For me, it's an endangered baseball park that'll soon celebrate its one hundredth birthday.

My father took me to Fenway for the first time in 1961, Yaz's rookie season, when I was eight years old. It was a night game against the Orioles and the Red Sox won. Later that season, I had an offer to go to Fenway for a doubleheader against the Tigers. It would be a long day, I was warned, and they didn't want any complaining or whining about leaving early. No problem. Sitting in the right field grandstand, I watched Al Kaline's back (he was number 6) for 18 innings.

For ten years I had to go into Boston once a year for asthma checkups at the old Lahey Clinic on Commonwealth Avenue. The reward was a Sox game at Fenway. It also taught me a lot about disappointment. There was nothing worse than rain on the day of our trip to Boston. Even now, unexpected disappointment reminds me of a Red Sox rainout on the day I went to Boston when I was twelve years old. On the brighter side, I still remember being fifteen and seeing Denny McLain win one of his 31 games in the summer of 1968. We sat in section 1 in right field. The worst seats in the house. Who cared? It was a part of baseball history—like getting to see Mark McGwire hit a home run in the summer of 1998.

When I finally got my driver's license, my friends and I would motor from Groton to the Riverside T lot on Route 128 in Newton. We'd hop on the Green Line inbound to the Fenway Park stop, then walk with the rest of the Sox legions to our hardball Mecca. Perfect. That way, we got to see night games at Fenway without having to drive in Boston. During those same years, I remember taking a school field trip to Boston for a Saturday game with the Oakland A's. The A's scored a million runs, and Reggie Jackson knocked home about ten with a flat-sided bat that was later ruled illegal. When I was a high school senior, I drove into Boston for a day game and invited a hometown girl who was studying at Simmons (conveniently located two blocks from Fenway). We sat in the bleachers and had to move every couple innings so she could maximize the sun's exposure on her face.

As a sophomore at Holy Cross, I went to Fenway with a bunch of fellow Crusaders in 1973 to see the Yankees and Red Sox. We saw Ron Blomberg and Orlando Cepeda make history as baseball's first designated hitters. During my college summers I was a legislative intern, and in those days the state representatives had Fenway passes, which enabled them to gain admission for fifty cents. My state rep gave me his pass, and I spent many a weekday afternoon studying John

Opening Day, 1956

Curtis and Rogelio Moret at the taxpayers' expense. It was there that I met a man, now a Massachusetts Superior Court judge, who told me that he used to grade bar exams sitting in the stands at Fenway. It still tickles me to think that there are lawyers in this state who possibly passed the bar because my friend was happy about a Jim Rice grand slam.

It wasn't until 1975 that I first walked into Fenway in any professional capacity. Standing on the field and in the dugout and seeing the clubhouses for the first time, I felt a new love for the old place. I wasn't going to play for the Red Sox, but I would begin my career in the old green ballyard where I'd spent so many days and nights with my family and friends.

As a quote runner for the Associated Press legend Dave O'Hara, I made seven dollars per game at Fenway in the summer of '75. It was probably the best job I ever had. Along with my best pal, Kevin Dupont, I got to eat dinner every night in the pressroom before games, then hang around and listen to the old-timers talk baseball long after the Red Sox had won or lost. It was in the old wooden Fenway pressroom that I intro-

More than any sport,

baseball is about generations.

— DAN SHAUGHNESSY

duced myself to Tom Yawkey, the owner of the Red Sox, who looked like the custodian, and had dinner with Jumpin' Joe Dugan, who had been Babe Ruth's roommate while playing third base for the 1927 New York Yankees. Dugan told me that I ate more than Ruth; probably I did. After all, the food was free, and I was in debt because of college loans. There were nights when Billy Martin waxed crude. Eyes wide, I listened to Dick O'Connell, Calvin Griffith, and Earl Weaver. I got to drink with the gods and soak up their stories and their hardball wisdom.

My status as an AP quote runner enabled me to buy tickets to the 1975 World Series at Fenway, so I was with my sister Ann in section 27 when Carlton Fisk clanged his home run for the ages in Game 6.

Section 27 is also where I saw my father for the last time, in September of 1979. We shared a handshake in the stands before I went to work, covering the Baltimore Orioles in the visitors' clubhouse. My dad died a month later, while I was covering the World Series in Baltimore. He was buried next to a Little League ball field in Pepperell, Massachusetts.

Each of my three children was born during baseball season, at Boston's Beth Israel Hospital, where some rooms have a view of Fenway Park. A few hours after my daughter, Kate, was born on July 30, 1985, I walked down to Fenway and handed out cigars to the writers behind the batting cage covering the Red Sox night game against the White Sox.

More than a decade later, I brought the kids to Fenway regularly. They complained about our crappy old cars, but never about the inconveniences of the ancient ballpark. We didn't mind standing every time the guy in the middle of our row had to go out to get another beer. We didn't mind the poles that occasionally obscured Nomar at short or Pedro on the mound. I still take some weird comfort in the knowledge that these poles are the same green beams that blocked the vision of my dad and his dad when they would take the trolley in from Cambridge to watch the Red Sox in the 1920s.

The old Boston Garden served as New England's indoor sports palace from 1928 to 1995 and came to be part of the identity of the Boston Bruins and Celtics. With small seats, obstructed views, smelly bathrooms, pitiful parking, zero air conditioning, tiny concessions, and loud fans who sat practically on top of the team benches, everything about the Garden was Boston. On television, in person, or even on the radio (the Garden had a distinct horn to signify the end of a period or quarter), you knew where the game was being played.

In the name of progress, air conditioning, and luxury boxes, the Garden went dark in the fall of 1995 and yielded to a generic arena built less than a foot from the old building and named after a bank. The New Garden has proven to be clean, expensive, air-conditioned, and completely soulless. Fans no longer have obstructed views, but they are so far back from the court or ice, they can barely make out the players' numbers. Forty-seven percent of the seats in the New Garden would fall outside the physical confines of the old building. The top row of the Old Garden was 105 feet from center court. The top row of the new building is 164 feet from the same spot. The distant fans certainly can't be heard. Watching a game at the New Garden is like watching a game in a bank. The bathrooms and concession stands are pristine and plentiful, and escalators and elevators assist fans in search of comfort, but there is nothing Boston about the place. The Bruins and Celtics have lost their home advantage. There is nothing memorable about the experience.

Because of the New Garden, concert promoters in Boston can now compete with the likes of Hartford, Springfield, Worcester, and Providence. Big deal. Elton John and Billy Joel no longer fear the acoustics of Boston's big arena, but the Montreal Canadiens and Los Angeles Lakers aren't afraid of the new building either. That's where Boston lost. The Old Garden had the ghosts and the glory, along with the heart and soul of our teams and our town.

Webb Nichols, an architect in Watertown, wrote in the *Globe*, "As a place of public assembly, a stadium or ballpark is an expression of the involvement of a community in the life and passion of the time. However, it is the game through which we bear our collective witness as a community. It is only the game that creates a common memory binding those who were there together. It is the experience of the game that is under assault."

Stan Grossfeld, the eyes of this book, grew up in the Bronx and got to watch the Mick in center field, beating the tar out of the Red Sox year after year when we were kids in the 1950s and '60s. Stan is a baseball guy. I have never seen him happier than when he personally thanked Fay Vincent, then commissioner, for suspending George Steinbrenner from baseball. Fortunately for those of us who love Fenway, Stan is now a card-carrying citizen of Red Sox Nation, and his affection for our park comes across in his photographs here.

Joe Wood warms up to an overflow crowd at Fenway in 1912, when fans sat within feet of the foul lines.

Previous page: Fenway, 1912

A religious shrine or a giant pinball machine? The House of Usher or a house of pain? Museum or amusement park? Historical or hysterical? The oldest park in the major leagues, the last of the single-deck baseball theaters, Fenway Park has inspired more lavish praise and outrageous comparison than any

American sports arena. New York's House That Ruth Built is certainly the ballpark most steeped in honor and history, but nobody ever compared Yankee Stadium to the Sistene Chapel. Perhaps Fenway is showered with torrents of purple prose because the park is in New England, the home of more poets, bards, pop psychologists, and writers than any American pocket.

The estimable John Updike dubbed it a "lyric little bandbox" and wrote that Fenway represents "a compromise between Man's Euclidean determinations and Nature's beguiling irregularities." The late, great House Speaker Tip O'Neill (born in 1912, the same year as Fenway) said, "It's like being in an English theatre. You're right on top of the stage. So chummy." Bill Lee called it "a shrine where people come for religious rites." The former Yankee manager Buck Showalter said, "I don't know anything about classical music, but if there's a baseball symphony, this is it." And to think that Mo Vaughn, the former Sox star, said, "Blow the damn place up."

Blow it up? That's precisely what happened in Cincinnati, Philadelphia, and Pittsburgh in the 1960s: Cincinnati's Crosley Field gave way to Riverfront Stadium. Philadelphia lost Connie Mack Stadium and got the Vet. Pittsburgh's charming Forbes Field was demolished and replaced by another spaceship cookie-cutter called Three

Rivers Stadium. It seemed like progress at the time, but now fans in all three cities long for the good old days and the good old ballparks. In the summer of '98, the Pirates announced plans to build a $228-million ballpark that'll remind fans of old Forbes Field. Everything old is new again—only more expensive.

THE RED SOX DID NOT ALWAYS PLAY THEIR HOME games at Fenway Park. Boston's charter American League franchise was formed in 1901, and the Huntington Grounds served quite nicely for the first eleven years of its history. Less than a mile from Fenway, at the corner of Huntington and Rogers avenues, the wood stadium was the site of the first World Series—won by the Red Sox (actually, they were the Pilgrims then) over the Pittsburgh Pirates in September 1903. Happily, the park was just a short walk from the watering hole of the immortal 'Nuff Ced McGreevey. 'Nuff Ced's bar was called Third Base because that's your last stop on the way home, and there fans gathered before and after games to drink and discuss baseball. Today the site of the Huntington Grounds is part of the campus of Northeastern University, and the only baseball memento is a statue of Cy Young and a plaque dedicated in 1993. The area certainly looks nothing like it did after the turn of the twentieth century, when it was owned by the New York, New Haven, and Hartford Railroad. There's no railyard soot gathering on the cap of the Cy Young statue.

That first park was built in less than two months in the spring of 1901, and the Pilgrims drew 289,448 in their inaugural season in the renegade American League. They finished first in 1903 and '04 and led the league in attendance with a whopping 623,295 (not including thousands of daily gate-crashers) in 1904.

In 1910 John I. Taylor, the owner of the Red Sox (a perk given to him by his dad, who owned the *Boston Globe*), decided not to renew his lease at the Huntington Grounds. The Taylor family was intent on selling the club and knew it could seek a higher price, and attract more bidders, if a ballpark was part of the deal. On June 24, 1911, Taylor announced his intention to build a new park for the Boston Red Sox (Taylor had snatched the new name when the crosstown Boston Nationals abandoned their carmine hose in favor of white stockings in 1907).

The *Boston Globe,* not surprisingly, provided exhaustive coverage for the announcement. It ran a half-page sketch of the proposed park and an accompanying story that concluded: "With the new park covering 365,306 square feet of land and the stands of the most approved type, and the home club brought up to its best pitch, the fans hereabouts can confidently look forward through the winter months to some great baseball games next season."

The plot of land for the new ballpark was in the Fenway area, between Lansdowne and Jersey streets. New trolley lines served the area and made it an appealing site for the Taylors. The Fenway had been a smelly mudflat until 1881–85, when it was drained as part of a plan to include it in the Emerald Necklace envisioned by Frederick Law Olmsted, the noted landscape architect. The area was Boston's last filled-in district, but the plan to make it part of the necklace was eventually scrapped.

Like the Red Sox and the *Globe,* the land for the new park was already owned by the Taylors; more specifically, by the Fenway Realty Company, another Taylor holding company. Taylor had purchased the land after buying the Red Sox in 1904. Part of Boston folklore is John I. Taylor's alleged reason for naming the field. His famous quote goes: "It's in the Fenway, isn't it? Then call it Fenway Park." That sounds nice, but in fact the name was intended to promote Fenway Realty.

Today, almost every modern sports palace (such as Coors Field, Pro Player Park, United Center, and Qualcomm) sells its name to the highest corporate bidder. The Pirates got $42 million from PNC Bank Corp. for the right to name their new stadium. The Red Sox no doubt will do the same thing. And when this happens, New England purists would do well to remember that Wrigley Field is named after chewing gum, and Fenway Park amounted to free publicity for the Taylors' realty company. If Boston's next baseball facility is named Century 21 Park, it would only be consistent with the Taylors' action in 1912.

Fenway Park was a land deal, nothing more. When construction was under way, the Taylors sold half their interest in the Red Sox for a reported $150,000, covering their original investment. They also retained ownership of the park. Sweet deal.

Before the ballpark was built, a church and the Park Riding School were the area's most visible structures. There was no Citgo sign, no Green Monster, no Pizzeria Uno in Kenmore Square.

The Red Sox broke ground on September 25, 1911, for one of the first steel and concrete parks in the world. The first known baseball park was the Brooklyn Grounds, built in 1862. The enclosed diamond had special benches for ladies and another section for gamblers. The outfield fences were 500 feet from home plate and, like every other park built before Fenway, it was made predominantly of wood. In an age when almost all the fans smoked, wood stadiums routinely caught fire. Ironically, although Fenway was built with considerable fireproof material, it would twice be damaged by fire before 1935.

Fenway was built by the Charles Logue Building Company; James E. McLaughlin was the chief architect, and the Osborn Engineering Company of Cleveland provided civil engineering services. Erected on 365,308 square feet of urban space, Fenway cost $650,000 to build, which was accomplished totally with private funding— no mention of personal seat licenses, luxury boxes, or state funding for infrastructure. Upon completion, the

The 1912 World Champion Red Sox. The team won 105 games during the season and beat the New York Giants in the World Series.

park was assessed at $420,000 (now about half of the average sale price of a home in Newton), the land at $344,000.

John I. Logue, a grandson of the man who built Fenway, wrote in 1995: "It's important to me and my extended family that my grandfather is known as the builder of the ballpark which is so prominent in the history of baseball. In the family records, we have a picture of Charles Logue with John Taylor, the Red Sox owner, and the Comiskey brothers, visiting from Chicago, at the Opening Day luncheon. However, the game was rained out."

In the intervening years there have been hundreds of changes, including obvious ones like light towers, bullpens, the giant video screen, the EMC Club, Monster Seats, new bathrooms, elevators, luxury suites, and an ATM machine under the first base grandstand. There was certainly no Legal Sea Food clam chowder on sale for four dollars in 1912, and it's doubtful that Tris Speaker called his agent from a cell phone in the home team's clubhouse. Even Jersey Street has been renamed (it's now Yawkey Way). But if you stand there and gaze up at the red brick of Fenway's main entrance, you are looking at the same facade that greeted fans attending the first exhibition game, between the Red Sox and Harvard, on April 9, 1912. The front of Fenway, patterned after Philadelphia's Shibe Park, is designed in a tapestried red brick Boston Colonial style, replete with diamond patterns, mosaics, and keystone arches. Like the main entrance to the Fairmont Copley Plaza Hotel, also built in 1912, the front of Fenway is frozen in time. It could be used to shoot a scene from *The Fitzgeralds and the Kennedys* and hold up quite well.

Much of the asymmetry that has made Fenway so charming and diabolical through the years can be attributed to Boston's crazy maze of streets and rail lines. Anyone who has driven in the Hub knows that the street pattern makes no sense, and Fenway's dimensions are directly related to this nightmare.

One doesn't need aerial photography to conclude that Boston has no standard grid design. Legend has it that many of the roads started out as cowpaths, which helps explain the city's geographic smorgasbord. Fenway Park is framed by Brookline Avenue, Yawkey Way,

The Royal Rooters, a band of everyday Sox fans, riot in 1912

Lansdowne Street, Ipswich Street, and Van Ness Street. This beast is no Pentagon, however, although the self-importance of some Red Sox offices might lead one to believe otherwise. It was Mo Vaughn who, in the spring of 1998, referred to John Harrington and Dan Duquette, CEO and general manager of the Sox respectively, as "the Joint Chiefs of Staff."

Even with its relatively small footprint, Fenway could have been symmetrical, but concessions to the street layout had to be made once the Taylor family called for team offices on the Jersey Street side. There was no thought of

when their seats are sold to other customers before the next-to-last game of the World Series.

night baseball in 1911, so the architects had to make sure batters would not be facing into the sun late in the afternoon. Thus home plate was set in the southwest corner of the yard (magnetic north is just a few degrees to the right of the left field line) to ensure that the sun would set behind third base, bothering only the right fielder. This meant that Lansdowne Street would be only a little more than 300 feet from home plate, so there would be no seating beyond the left field fence. Lansdowne Street was banked on its far side by the Boston & Albany Railroad. Since the Sox couldn't move outward, they eventually

moved up (the skyscraper syndrome), and so the Green Monster was born. More on that later. Much more.

The placement of the outfield fences was not a big issue in 1912. It was the deadball era, and players were not hitting the ball 350 feet. The fences were supposed to eliminate gate-crashing and free looks from the street. Today, league rules govern field dimensions (the fences in new parks must be at least 325 feet from home plate), but one of the beauties of baseball parks is that each one has its own dimensions. Football and basketball share none of this—fields and courts are "regulation." Hockey had some

Fenway Park was first used for football by the Boston Redskins in the 1930s.

unique rinks through the years (the Boston Garden had a notoriously small ice surface and the Bruins built their teams accordingly), but baseball was the sport with fields like snowflakes—no two were alike. Thanks in part to its fences, Boston's park is an architectural mutant.

Fenway was not quite complete when the Red Sox beat Harvard, 2–0, in its first exhibition game. Sod had been transplanted from the Huntington Grounds, but there were no right field bleachers yet and only a small section of seats in center. The area beyond right field was roped off for parking. (The rest of the bleachers were not added until the Sox made it to the 1912 World Series.) The event did not attract the 10,000 men of Harvard. Only 3,000 fans attended the weather-shortened (snow flurries in April) exhibition game against the Johnnies.

The park's first American League game, against the New York Highlanders, was scheduled for April 18, but rain pushed it back to Saturday, April 20. By that time not as many people cared. The *Titanic* had gone down on April 15, and the Cunard liner *Carpathia* arrived in New York with survivors the day before the game. Naturally, there was little talk of baseball, as newspapers scrambled for any and all information about the disaster. The day after Fenway opened, it got two paragraphs on the front page of the *Boston Globe*. The headline SOX OPEN TO PACKED PARK was dwarfed by THRICE WARNED, a survivor's chilling account of three iceberg warnings that were allegedly transmitted from the crow's nest of the *Titanic* to the officer on the steamship's bridge.

The Red Sox won the opener, beating New York, 7–6, in 11 innings. Admission was twenty-five cents for the bleachers, fifty cents for the pavilion. Tris Speaker knocked home the winning run. Throwing out the first ball was Boston's mayor, John "Honey Fitz" Fitzgerald. Again, Fenway was awash in history—past, present, and future. Not only was the ballpark dedicated in the same week the *Titanic* sank, but the first pitch was hurled by the grandfather-to-be of John F. Kennedy. Our thirty-fifth president was not born until five years later.

Fenway Park had the first electric scoreboard, a curious feature in 1912, and 18 turnstiles, more than any ballpark in the majors. Fans could get there easily: it was a short walk from Kenmore Square and near the Ipswich Street trolley line. There were some complaints about the bleachers being too far from the action, but the park was well received in most initial reports.

In the early years, the Red Sox almost could not lose at their new home field. The 1912 Red Sox edition (still known as "the Speed Boys" in many accounts), went 57–20 at home and beat the New York Giants in 7 games to win the World Series. They hit only 29 homers, however, 6 fewer than they hit a year earlier at the Huntington Grounds. Two years later, the National League Boston Braves borrowed Fenway for the World Series and beat the Philadelphia A's in four straight. The Sox won the World Series again in 1915, 1916 (though these were played at the new Braves Field, which was larger), and 1918. Yankee Stadium still hadn't been built, but it certainly seemed as though Fenway was going to be the home of champions for a long time. When Babe Ruth hurled Boston to a Series victory over the Cubs in 6 games in 1918, the park was only seven years old but had already been the home of four championship teams and had served as the World Series site for another. Who knew that that was going to be it for the remainder of the century?

Meanwhile, the ballpark had an impact on the city. The site was originally considered part of Boston's perimeter, but the neighborhood expanded in the early years of the park to become a prime residential and commercial district. Fenway Park was the catalyst for this urban development, like an early Camden Yards or Jacobs Field.

Today, baseball purists are horrified by the sacrilegious giant Coke bottles on the left field light tower, but there is plenty of tacky precedent. Early pictures of Fenway show a much smaller left field wall plastered with advertisements for whiskey, razor blades, and soap.

Fenway was the third-largest park in the country when it opened, but there were still some overflow crowds; when this happened, the management simply put ropes in the outfield and let the fans sit behind the Sox outfielders. The 10-foot-high sloped area in front of the left field wall (named Duffy's Cliff because of the talent of the Sox left fielder Duffy Lewis) was especially popular because it afforded the best view. Putting fans behind the rope called for some interesting ground rules, but none like the ones laid down after the first Fenway fire, in 1926. The May blaze wiped out the bleachers along the left field foul line; the section was not repaired for almost a decade.

The sale of Babe Ruth to the Yankees in the winter of 1919–20 has been well documented, and Boston's baseball fans still lament the deal, blaming eighty-six years of subsequent bad luck on the Curse of the Bambino. It's a nifty, superstition-over-science theme and conveniently explains eight decades of disappointment and near misses, but it's often forgotten that the beloved Boston ballpark was also part of the deal. Sad but true. Harry Frazee, the owner of the Sox, sent Ruth to Jacob Ruppert, the Yankees' owner, for $125,000 and a $350,000 loan for a mortgage on Fenway. So not only did the Sox lose the greatest player in baseball history, but their home field was owned by the hated Yankees until 1933, when a thirty-year-old millionaire, Thomas A. Yawkey, bought the team from Bob Quinn, the owner since 1926. It's no wonder that the Red Sox kept sending good players to New York after Ruth was sold. The Yankees' owner was Boston's landlord, and dear Fenway was Frazee's hardball collateral. When Yawkey bought the team, he asked Ruppert to carry the note for another year, but everything changed when the Red Sox beat the Yanks five straight times in 1933. Ruppert demanded full payment and Yawkey cut him a check at once, restoring the independence and dignity of Fenway Park.

Yawkey's next move was to renovate the park. At the end of the 1933 season, the young Boston owner sank more than a million Depression dollars into the rebuilding. There was a discouraging setback after New Year's

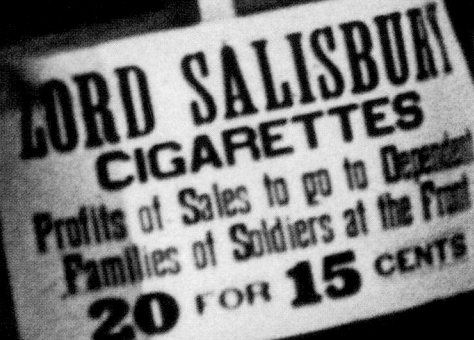

The Babe — a member of the Red Sox from 1914 to 1919 — visits with kids on his return as a Yankee.

Previous page: Well-dressed vendors hawk cigarettes outside Fenway Park during World War I.

Day when Boston's worst fire in twelve years beset Fenway. Yawkey's response was to replace the wooden stands in center field with concrete bleachers. He also ripped out the wooden seats in left and right field, extended the bleachers to the left field wall, built new seating in right field, added 6,000 grandstand seats, and built the press box, which lasted until 1989. In all, 15,708 new seats were installed to make Fenway's official capacity 37,500, the sixth largest in baseball. Yawkey even had workers sandblast the Jersey Street entrance. Fenway sparkled again.

Yawkey's home renovation also gave birth to the single most important element of Fenway Park, the Green Monster. Duffy's Cliff was dug up and replaced by a 37-foot-high fence of sheet metal and steel. Two years later a 23-foot-high screen—designed to save baseballs and protect windows on Lansdowne Street—was added to the top of the fence.

It is impossible to overstate what the Wall means to Fenway. It has changed the way the Red Sox play baseball, sometimes saving them, but more often killing them

(hello, Bucky Dent). It would be difficult to find another sports arena with a feature as famous as Fenway's Green Monster. Yankee Stadium has monument park and one portion of the famous upper-deck facade, but neither compares with Fenway's Monster.

If the Sox were to leave Fenway, they'd certainly want to build another Wall in any new park. New York's owner George Steinbrenner faced the same dilemma when he rebuilt Yankee Stadium in 1973. The upper-deck facade was the park's signature fixture, but because of its weight, it was impossible to make it part of the renovated park (which has no poles).

"In 1970, the facade went all around the stadium," remembered Steinbrenner. "In 1973, I was sitting with a dear friend of mine, who has now passed—Terry Grant. He was a great baseball fan. We were pals and we'd sit in those old boxes and they were going to redo the whole stadium. He asked what we were going to do with the facade that made the stadium familiar to everybody. I didn't know and I called the engineer and he said we had no plans for it. Terry was an artistic guy and he told me that the beauty of that could not be lost. The new overhangs wouldn't take the weight, so we put some piece of it in center field and it's still there today."

Wrigley Field's ivy outfield walls probably come closest to matching Fenway's Monster monument. And Chicago's buildings across Waveland Avenue beyond Wrigley's left field fence might be compared with Boston's towering Citgo sign—which has inspired at least one song and a three-minute movie. The sign looms over the Green Monster and serves as an unofficial Boston monument, not unlike the eyes of Dr. Eckelberg in F. Scott Fitzgerald's *Great Gatsby*. The Citgo sign was built in 1965 and went dark during the energy crisis of the late 1970s, but it was rescued when sentimental citizens petitioned the Boston Landmarks Commission. Renovated in 1983, it serves as an ever-present distant cousin to the Green Monster.

With the Wall in place and the rest of the park fully renovated (losing more foul territory behind home plate), Yawkey gave Boston fans in 1934 the park we know today. In 2007, some seats in Fenway provide a view virtually identical to the one you would have had in the summer of

1934. The poet Donald Hall wrote: "We love baseball because it seizes and retains the past, like the snowy village inside a glass paperweight." That is what Fenway does for us as it ushers in another century of major league baseball in Boston.

The bullpens were added in 1940, after Ted Williams's rookie season. The pens gave the relief pitchers a sanctuary from the sidelines and moved the right field fences 23 feet closer to home plate. Oddly enough, Williams's homer total went from 31 to 23 the year after the bullpens were installed, but Teddy Ballgame and every lefty who came after him eventually took advantage of the cozier dimensions.

The bullpens are fan favorites. Right field is where young fans have a chance to engage in conversation with pitchers and catchers from both teams. Bill Lee always had a lot of fun with the bleacher creatures, and Bob Stanley delighted the masses by smashing beachballs with a bullpen rake. Dennis Eckersley, who first came to Fenway in 1975 and returned to the Red Sox in '98, still speaks of "smelling weed" from his perch in the bullpen. The Oriole pitcher Ross Grimsley was involved in one of the more controversial bullpen moments when he fired a ball at a heckling fan in the 1970s. Trying to scare the fan, he threw the ball at a protective screen, but the baseball somehow penetrated the screen, struck the fan, and provoked a lawsuit.

In 1963, Cleveland's right fielder Al Luplow made what is considered the greatest catch in Fenway history when he took a home run away from the Sox's pinch-hitter Dick Williams. Luplow jumped over the wall and caught Williams's fly ball before landing in the Red Sox bullpen. Seattle's Jay Buhner made a more stationary leap and catch, landing in the bullpen to snatch a homer from Scott Hatteberg in 1997.

Fenway's right field line features a yellow foul pole stationed a hideous 302 feet from home plate. It is affectionately known as Pesky's Pole, named after the lovable Sox shortstop who claims to have curled 8 of his 17 career homers inside it. Carl Yastrzemski ripped a short homer down the line against rocketman Ron Guidry in the 1978 playoff game, but most of the cheapie round-trippers to this corner are hit by banjo right-handed hit-ters who get behind a fastball and slice it down the line.

The measurement for Pesky's Pole is deceiving because the wall tapers dramatically, and straightaway right field is a more serious 380 feet from home plate. Left-handed hitters have a hard time driving the ball out in right field, particularly in the spring, when the east wind cuts to the bone.

Beyond the right field fence, far up the bleachers, a single red seat—seat 21 in row 37 of section 42—sits in a sea of green. Known simply as "the red seat," it marks the spot where Ted Williams hit the longest measured home run in Fenway's history. Like a fleck of red paint on an otherwise lush green canvas, the commemorative chair draws the eye. Someone is almost always sitting there, even when just a few patrons are in the bleachers. When new fans ask about it, the citizens of Red Sox Nation are happy to relay the Fenway folklore. Teddy Ballgame's mighty clout was struck on a windy, sun-splashed Sunday afternoon in 1946 in the first inning of the second game of a doubleheader against the Tigers.

"Hell, I can tell you everything about that one," Williams said when asked about it. "I hit it off Fred Hutchinson, who was a tough rightie who changed speeds real good. Let me tell ya—changing speeds didn't bother me nearly that much. I could pick up the movement of his arm. He threw me a changeup and I saw it coming. I picked it up fast and I just whaled into it."

The ball sailed over the head of Detroit's right fielder Pat Mullin, then carried beyond the visitors' bullpen and kept on going to crash down on top of Joseph A. Boucher's head. More accurately, it landed on Boucher's straw hat, puncturing the middle of the fashionable skimmer. Boucher was a construction engineer from Albany who lived in an apartment on Commonwealth Avenue when he worked in Park Square during the week. Sitting more than thirty rows behind the bullpen, he wasn't expecting to catch any home run balls on that fateful June afternoon.

Scratching his head, after the game Boucher asked the *Globe*'s Harold Kaese, "How far away must one sit to be safe in this park? I didn't even get the ball. They say it bounced a dozen rows higher, but after it hit my

Larry Doby, the first black player in the American League, examines a billboard at Fenway promoting racial harmony.

head, I was no longer interested. I couldn't see the ball. Nobody could. The sun was right in our eyes. All we could do was duck. I'm glad I didn't stand up."

The next day's *Globe* featured a page 1 photo of Boucher holding his hat, his finger stuck through the hole. The caption read, "BULLSEYE!..."

Newspaper accounts claimed that Williams's homer traveled 450 feet, but the Red Sox measured the distance in the mid-1980s and arrived at an official count of 502 feet. This doesn't take into account where the ball would have landed had it not been stopped by Boucher's head.

"It's hard to believe anybody could hit a ball that

far," said Mo Vaughn, himself a slugger. "I know I've never even come close—not even in batting practice. I mean, it's not even down the line. It's in the gap! You can barely see that thing."

In 1984, the Sox owner Haywood Sullivan decided to commemorate Williams's clout by putting a red plastic seat in the spot where Boucher sat on June 9, 1946. Boucher's grandson, William McGuire of Quincy, said, "You never would find a more devoted Red Sox fan than my grandfather. When he didn't go home to Albany on weekends, he always went to Fenway Park. I used to hop on the train and go meet him when I was a kid. If they ever tear down Fenway, I want first dibs on that seat."

Vern Stephens and Walt Dropo with a bevy of beauties, ca. 1950

Seven light towers were erected in 1947 when the Red Sox—ever on the cutting edge—became the fourteenth of the sixteen big league teams to play at night. The Red Sox beat the White Sox, 5–3, on June 13, 1947, in Fenway's first night game. In 1953, Yawkey built a runway between the visitors' dugout and the clubhouse. Until then, both teams had entered and exited through a single tunnel, but the system failed when the combustible Billy Martin and even more combustible Jimmy Piersall duked it out after a game in May 1952.

The garage door in foul territory in left field, big enough to accommodate car traffic, has survived several renovations. It stays closed during games, but fair balls hit down the left field line sometimes wind up rattling around the door frame. The players, coaches, and managers in the visitors' dugout (near third base) and fans in the left field grandstand cannot see what is happening when a left fielder disappears into the corner to joust with a baseball bouncing around the door frame. Only at Fenway.

Fenway's center field flagpole was removed from the warning track in 1970, and padding was installed on the outfield walls after the rookie wonderboy Fred Lynn crashed into the center field fence during the 1975 World Series. The electronic mega-scoreboard was installed in 1976, and forty-four luxury boxes were built, starting in 1982.

Fenway is one of the last major league parks still featuring organ music before and after games and between innings. Most parks have succumbed to ear-splitting rock 'n' roll, bombarding the senses with endless replays of "Louie Louie" and "Twist and Shout." Fenway introduced rock 'n' roll in the 1990s, but the Rolling Stones and the Beatles share time with a Yamaha Electone organ. The late John Kiley manned the Fenway organ for three decades, and veteran fans still get chills when they remember Kiley's bursting into the Hallelujah Chorus after Carlton Fisk's home run off the foul pole in Game 6 of the 1975 World Series. Today Red Sox fans hear an assortment of rock music throughout the game, and before the home half of the eighth inning the sellout crowd sings along while Neil Diamond's "Sweet Caroline" blares from the sound system. When the Sox win, fans hear "Dirty Water" by the Standells.

The last true bleacher seats—wooden planks with no backs—were replaced with plastic seats in 1983, the same year that Fenway's first elevator was built. In 1989, the old press box was gutted to make room for the infamous 600 Club behind home plate, and a new press box was built on top of the 600 Club, giving sportswriters a perch 100 feet above the batter's box—a vantage point normally associated with the Goodyear blimp.

The left field wall and the outfield dimensions are always cited when Fenway is portrayed as a hitter's ballpark, but the lack of foul territory may contribute as much as the cozy fences. A pop-up that would be an out in Oakland is out of play in Fenway. The Fenway hitter lives for another pitch. Over the course of 81 games, this inflates batting averages and RBI totals. It's a double benefit for fans: their proximity to the players contributes to the high-scoring games by eliminating extra outs.

In 1958, Ted Williams was reminded once again just how close the fans are. After striking out against the Washington Senator righty Bill Fischer (later a pitching coach with the 1986 World Series Red Sox), Williams took a vicious cut at an imaginary ball and the bat slipped from his hands. It sailed into the air and crashed down on the head of sixty-nine-year-old Gladys Heffernan, who was sitting in the front row near the Sox dugout. Fortunately, Heffernan was the housekeeper of Joe Cronin, the general manager of the Red Sox, and did not sue Williams or the team.

Fenway has spawned imitators, none more authentic than Bucky Dent's "Little Fenway," off Linton Boulevard next to U.S. 1 in Delray Beach, Florida. Built almost to scale (without 33,000 seats) in 1988–89, Dent's mini-Fenway is the centerpiece of his baseball school, but it also serves as a cruel joke on Red Sox Nation. The numbers on the Little Fenway left field scoreboard represent one of the worst days in Red Sox history, October 2, 1978. It shows the Yankees leading the Red Sox, 3–2, with New York batting in the top of the seventh inning—the moment just before Dent's three-run pop-fly homer off Mike Torrez ruined Boston's best team of the last half century. On February 13, 1989, Dent imported Torrez for the grand opening of the Fenway replica. Torrez gleefully cooperated, going so far as to throw Dent another gopher ball to christen the park. Dent hit another homer off Torrez. "I'd like to thank Mike Torrez one more time," he told the appreciative crowd. "Without him, none of this would have been possible."

Ouch. It was like watching the captain of the *Exxon Valdez* ramming his oil tanker into shore a second time.

Meanwhile, closer to home, the former Red Sox third baseman Tim Naehring wants to build a $1.5-million replica of Fenway Park on twelve acres next to a landfill in Quincy, Massachusetts. Run by Naehring's Athletes Reaching Out Foundation, it would provide a free ball field for Little League and high school teams. If you're looking for a scaled-down model, there's a

I don't know anything about

classical music,

but if there's a baseball symphony,

this is it.

— BUCK SHOWALTER

company in Connecticut that will send you an official replica of Fenway Park for $47.50, payable in two monthly installments.

Small wonder that it has spawned imitators. Fenway Park is a friendly neighborhood joint, the corner bar of American sports palaces. The buildings around Fenway are old, the streets cracked, and the stores cater to students and baseball fans. On game day, it feels like a European marketplace outside the park, and the smells whet the appetite for what lies inside. Vendors sell all variety of sausage, chicken, and beef sandwiches. Carnival barkers promote their wares—"Peanuts! Programs! Souvenirs! Sunglasses! Baseball cards! Hot sausages!"—and every fan is assured that the price outside beats the one within Fenway's walls. It's the same with the saloons that rim the park on Yawkey Way, Brookline Ave., and Lansdowne Street. The beer at the Cask & Flagon is sure to be cheaper and richer than the watered-down six-dollar cup sold inside the yard.

IT'S BEEN POPULAR TO TALK ABOUT BASEBALL AS A country game, a sport played by boys in hamlets across America. In New England's factory and mill towns, the game certainly flourished when the teams in neighboring towns would compete, giving folks some cheap summer entertainment. In the 1930s, New England town baseball was as popular as concerts at the town bandstand. Coupled with the fable that the game was invented in little Cooperstown, New York, baseball looks like a Norman Rockwell magazine cover. There is much legitimacy to the image when one talks about the amateur and even minor league levels of professional baseball. But the big league game was made for and played in big cities. And that is why Fenway Park will always be better than The (new) Ballpark in Arlington, Texas, and the renovated Edison Field in Anaheim, California. Today's new parks in Baltimore, Cleveland, and Detroit are special because they still have the city skyline as a backdrop. They can be reached by subways and buses. They are only a short walk from the downtown hotels. They are part of city neighborhoods, like the old ballparks in Chicago, Pittsburgh, New York, and Philadelphia.

Fenway, surrounded by Boston's medical community and educational institutions, is a city park like none other. From the top of a Fenway light tower, one can see Children's Hospital and the Dana-Farber Cancer Institute, MIT and Harvard, the Massachusetts State House and the Charles River, the Museum of Fine Arts and Symphony Hall, and the old Braves Field, now part of Boston University. One can see the Bunker Hill Monument and Bunker Hill Community College, where Sacco and Vanzetti were executed in 1927, when it was the Charlestown State Prison. One can see the former Hotel Shelton, where Eugene O'Neill died, and Massachusetts Avenue, where Martin Luther King, Jr., lived when he studied at Boston University Divinity School. One can see Simmons, Emmanuel, and Wheelock colleges.

The best part about Fenway is that all of these places can be reached by foot. The worst part is that Fenway is almost impossible to find by car unless you are a veteran Hub driver. Many a Boston rookie—or a player acquired in a trade—has driven 'round and 'round the streets of Boston in a futile search for Fenway. Out-of-towners and once-a-year fans experience the same frustration. It's especially galling when one can see the ballpark but still can't move any closer to the promised land. Traveling east on the Mass. Turnpike, a driver sees the Green Monster to his right and can actually tell who's batting by looking at the giant scoreboard in center, but there is no specific exit for Fenway. One disappears into a tunnel and sees that the next exit is Copley Square. A first-time ticket holder from the suburbs instantly knows the feeling experienced by the legendary Charlie on the MTA. You can ride forever on the streets of Boston and never stumble over the famous Red Sox playground.

If you can get your car near Fenway, you still have to face your biggest hurdle: parking. Perhaps the field should be renamed Fenway No-Park because there is no place to beach your car. The Red Sox ballplayers use a tiny lot on Van Ness Street, right outside the Sox clubhouse, but the little lot can't accommodate the twenty-five Jeeps and Land Rovers driven by Papi and the gang, so the City of Boston allows the team to absorb Van Ness Street on game days. It's an old-

Ted Williams, Eddie Pellagrini, and Tiger slugger Hank Greenberg talk baseball with young congressional candidate John F. Kennedy in 1946.

fashioned "wink-wink" deal between the ball club and the Boston Police. Signs inform would-be parkers that meters around Fenway are not good two hours before and after a game. Cars that violate the order are either ticketed or towed. Most fans opt for space at nearby gas stations and fast food outlets, which become Sox parking lots on game days.

There is much about Fenway that is difficult to embrace, yet baseball fans flock to Yawkey Way year after year. To satisfy tourists who visit Boston in the off-season or when the Sox are out of town, the ball club provides official tours of Fenway. When the Sox are down in the standings, they stay up in attendance because Boston has a star ballpark.

Even the players, never a sentimental lot, remember Fenway fondly. Take Bill Buckner, for example. If ever there was a major leaguer who had reason to despise Fenway, it would be Buckner. He's a former All-Star, a batting champion, and collected 2,715 big league hits—but he is remembered only as the man who let a ground ball slither through his legs in Game 6 of the 1986 World Series. Buckner tried to raise a family in Greater Boston after he retired, but too often he was ridiculed for muffing the Little League grounder. He eventually settled in Meridian, Idaho, where he bought a car dealership and worked in real estate. His first real estate project was a subdivision of starter homes, which he named—what else?—Fenway Park.

On July 13, 1999, the All-Star Game visited Fenway Park for the third time in the ballyard's history. It was a three-day festival celebrating the national pastime and its roots in the hardball hub of the universe. For Red Sox fans, club officials, and baseball America, this figured to be the beginning of Fenway's long goodbye.

The Sox had already unveiled plans for a new Fenway, which included tearing down the existing structure. The 1999 All-Star Game looked like it was going to serve as the last hurrah for the oldest and most beloved ballpark in the major leagues.

The home run derby, annually cited by many fans as more exciting than the All-Star Game itself, took place on the Monday night of Boston's All-Star week, and Mark McGwire and Sammy Sosa were among the sluggers who wowed the Fenway faithful and an entire nation with prodigious blasts over the Green Monster. Fenway's showcase came just one year after the historic events of 1998: Cal Ripken Jr.'s consecutive-game streak and the McGwire-Sosa home run chase brought baseball back from the abyss after the damaging work stoppage of 1994.

Fenway's home run derby did not disappoint. Perhaps its only drawback was the inability to measure the monstrous shots hit over the Wall. Many balls peppered the garage roof across Landsdowne Street, and one of McGwire's blasts is believed to have one-hopped the rooftop and bounded onto the eastbound lane of the Massachusetts Turnpike.

One night later, Ted Williams was feted in a pregame ceremony on the Fenway lawn. Folks who wanted to pay their respect to Fenway had a chance to say goodbye to

Ted. It was Teddy Ballgame's final appearance at his old home office (Williams died on July 5, 2002). The best ballpark and the best hitter were going out together, it seemed.

The Splendid Splinter was wheeled onto the warning track in a golf cart driven by groundskeeper Al Forrester, who was part of the Fenway crew back when Williams played. The cart rolled to the pitcher's mound, where Ted—with help from Tony Gwynn—threw out the ceremonial first pitch to Carlton Fisk. After the toss, Ted was surrounded by members of both All-Star squads, plus dozens of Hall of Famers who had gathered in Boston to promote Major League Baseball's All-Century team. The unscripted demonstration of love for Teddy Ballgame caused the pregame ceremony to run long, which inflicted great pain on network television and its sponsors. This produced the hideous sight of MLB officials trying to move things along (toward the next commercial) while Williams was embraced by his baseball brotherhood. Then came perhaps the most ridiculous public address announcement in the history of ballparks when the man behind the microphone upstairs bellowed, "Would the greatest players of all time please clear the field?"

That means you, Bob Feller! You too, Willie Mays!

The game itself, a pedestrian, 4–1 American League

victory, was quite forgettable, save for two innings of Koufax-like pitching from Red Sox righty Pedro Martinez, who was then at the height of his powers. In a performance reminiscent of Carl Hubbell's dominance at the Polo Grounds in 1934, Pedro fanned five batters in his short stint and walked away with MVP honors.

It's hard to believe today, considering the improvements that have been made since the new owners purchased the team in 2002, but the Sox truly were committed to leaving Fenway when the baseball world gathered in Boston in the summer of 1999. It was inevitable, we were told. Red Sox CEO John Harrington had laid out the plan. The Sox were going to build a new ballpark next to the Fenway site. The blueprint called for a new version of the old park while leaving a portion of the original Fenway as a mini-museum for nostalgia buffs. This plan truly never had a chance. The Sox owned none of the considerable acreage that they would need to build the new park. They apparently were planning on the city's help in the form of an eminent domain land grab. A couple of the actual landowners quickly voiced their objections, and even though some civic funding was approved, the project remained in the blueprint phase right up until the old administration sold the ballclub in the winter of 2001–2002.

The new ownership group was led by billionaire John Henry, a quiet man who'd grown up listening to radio broadcasts of St. Louis Cardinals games. A low-talking, rarely visible owner, Henry had a great reverence for baseball history. The nocturnal number-cruncher who preferred e-mail to human contact, Henry had a soft spot for old Fenway Park. He was not in a hurry to tear down the past.

Henry enlisted the help of Larry Lucchino to carry out the daily business of running the ballclub and Fenway Park. Lucchino had overseen a baseball renaissance in Baltimore, culminating when Camden Yards was built in 1992. Without exaggeration, it can be stated that Camden Yards had a greater impact on baseball than anything else since Jackie Robinson broke the color barrier in 1947. Paying homage to the past while providing modern amenities, Baltimore's new ballpark changed the way parks were built. The last big-league park before Camden was Chicago's new Comiskey, and folks in the City of Big Shoulders blundered badly, building a ballyard similar to the dreadful dual-purpose doughnuts that polluted the National League in the 1960s—Veterans Stadium (Philadelphia), Shea Stadium (New York), Jack Murphy Stadium (San Diego), Riverfront Stadium (Cincinnati), Fulton County Stadium (Atlanta), Three Rivers Stadium (Pittsburgh), and Busch Stadium (St. Louis). The new Comiskey wasn't a cookie-cutter, but it was close. It was too steep, too big, and too much like the mistakes of the 1960s. It was also in a neighborhood with nothing to offer game day commuters.

Then came Camden Yards. All brick and exposed (green) steel beams, replete with odd angles and asymmetry, it demonstrated the best of old and new. It was a baseball park, not a stadium. It was within walking distance of Baltimore's beautiful, revitalized Inner Harbor. It paid homage to the birthplace of Babe Ruth and incorporated an ancient warehouse into part of the right field horizon. It changed the way all future ballparks were built, and it was the brainchild of the same two people who would be in charge of the upgrade and ultimate renovation of Fenway Park in the twenty-first century: Lucchino and Janet Marie Smith.

Larry Lucchino grew up in Pittsburgh and spent a

good portion of his youth at Forbes Field, the brick and ivy ballyard in the Oakland section of Steeltown where Bill Mazeroski hit the walkoff homer that beat the Yankees in the seventh game of the 1960 World Series. Lucchino was an accomplished second baseman for Allderdice High School before going to Princeton, where he played basketball with Bill Bradley. He never forgot the ballpark of his hardscrabble youth.

Janet Marie Smith grew up in Jackson, Mississippi, the daughter of an architect. She was thirty-five years old when Camden Yards was finished, and through the years there have been differing versions regarding who should get the lion's share of the credit for the revolutionary ballyard. Two full-blown books are devoted to the subject, and Smith and Lucchino are generally cited as the visionaries behind the project. Smith was later involved in the design of Atlanta's Turner Field.

When Lucchino found himself the CEO of the Boston Red Sox in 2002, it did not take him long to bring Smith on board. The mother of three children and by then a mini-celebrity in her new hometown of Baltimore, she jumped at the opportunity to work part-time in Boston: she would be in charge of the renovation and improvement of the most famous baseball park in America. For Smith, it was like being commissioned to oversee the restoration of the Mona Lisa.

That is why we have a new-old Fenway Park. In the early years of the Henry-Werner-Lucchino administration, the Sox were careful not to talk about ballpark "renovation." While dramatic changes were being made, careful language was used, and the Sox talked only of ballpark "improvement." The new administration was allegedly still exploring the idea of a new ballpark, and there was no formal commitment to old Fenway. But their intentions were obvious even to casual observers. They were spending millions on the old ballpark. You don't invest that kind of money in a house you plan to demolish. It was clear that they had no designs on building a new park. The Henry group decided early that expanding and improving Fenway was the best way to maximize revenues. The new owners had neither the land, the local connections, nor the ready cash that was needed for a new ballpark. It would have amounted to years of agonizing battles with neighbors, landowners, banks, and politicians. It would have crushed a growing grassroots legion of fans committed to saving old Fenway. Most important, it would have cost hundreds of millions of dollars.

And so the Henry group began the process of improving Fenway. They gradually, carefully altered the face of the ballyard, dramatically improved the fan experience, and (again most important for the ownership) sucked every possible dollar from a consumer base that was willing to pay any price for a day at Fenway Park.

It all started with "Henrytown," two rows of dugout seats that were added in front of the existing front row on the infield side of both dugouts. The new seats gobbled up more of the precious foul territory (not a friend of pitchers, Fenway already had less foul space than any ballpark in the majors) and put many fans closer to home plate than the man on the mound was. Amazing, but true. In Fenway's front row behind the screen, you are less than 60 feet, 6 inches, from home plate. John Henry's box is next to the Sox dugout, and the owner's private seat has a television screen that allows him to view replays of the action. His proximity also allows him to chat with the Sox manager or batting coach.

The new front row seats were wildly expensive ($300 per chairback in 2006), but no one objected. High rollers fought to get them. There was some initial concern that more fans might be injured by line drives off the end of the bat, but there's been no evidence of a spike in foul ball injuries. Every now and then a foul ball that would have been an out drops into the second row of Henrytown, and batters are eternally grateful for the new life. It's inevitable that someday a player will hit a game-winning, Fisk-like homer in October after hitting a popup that would have been an out in the old days. Imagine if Bucky Dent's homer had come after a foul pop that would have been caught if not for the seats installed. Henrytown was critical for two reasons. It demonstrated that there was an insatiable appetite for all things Fenway; the new owners learned that there was no backlash when they spiked prices or invented new high-end opportunities for Red Sox fans. Second, the new seats were remarkable because they were seamlessly incorporated into the old ballpark.

Those columns are your friends.

— JANET MARIE SMITH

Janet Marie Smith

After one or two games, even the purists forgot they were there. You couldn't tell where the new section ended and the old rows began. This was the first indication that the new owners knew what they were doing with ballpark changes. The old regime's last "change" was the tacky addition of hideous, gigantic Coca-Cola bottles strapped to the light towers on top of the Green Monster in 1997. Continuing with the Macy's parade theme, John Harrington and his friends put a giant Hood Milk bottle on top of the right field roof. Had the franchise not been sold, we no doubt would have the Stay-Puft Marshmallow Man in center.

The clever new owners were no less greedy than the old regime, but they were much more reverent and tasteful. When signage was added to the top of the Green Monster in the summer of 2002, it was sold as a return to the old days, when the Wall was a billboard featuring ads for whiskey, razor blades, and Lifebuoy Soap. Today Fenway has more signage than most NASCAR races, but there's little complaint. Everything is for sale. You can buy your way to throwing out a first pitch or announcing "Play ball." You can tour Fenway for $12. You can rent pri-

vate clubs for bar mitzvas or weddings. You could even buy a patch of championship sod after the 2004 World Series win.

It didn't take Janet Marie Smith long to make plans for Fenway once the new owners closed on the purchase in February of 2002. She would walk about the park, pen and clipboard in hand, making notes, poking at the underbelly, and finding inventive ways to make space, create a better game day experience, and spend Henry's millions. In September of 2002 the Sox unveiled their Gate A concourse expansion inside Yawkey Way—the oldest section of the ballpark. Fans noted the improved concessions and restrooms. The area was cleaner and more spacious. And it was only the beginning.

Fenway Park made national news on Opening Day 2003 when three rows of seats on top of the Green Monster were unveiled. It marked the most significant change to the ballpark since . . . the addition of bullpens ("Williamstown" in 1940)? . . . the addition of light towers in 1947?

Roger Clemens claims that he suggested putting seats on top of the Wall back in the 1980s, but when he raised

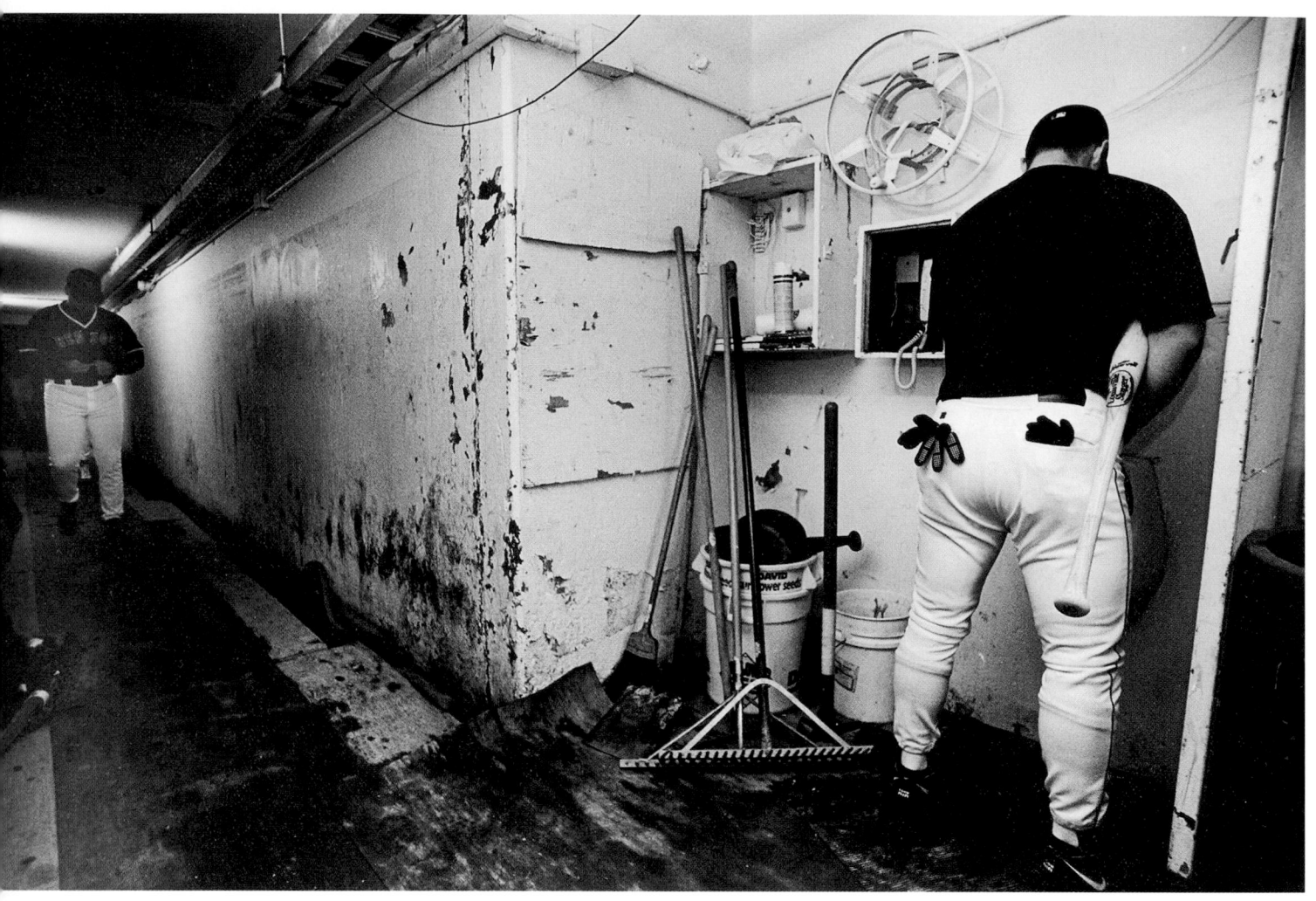

Fenway probably has the same urinals, though.

That's about the only thing that hasn't changed.

They're the same troughs that guys were using in the old days.

— GEORGE STEINBRENNER

Red Sox catcher Scott Hatteberg uses the facilities in the old runway
that connected the dugout to the clubhouse. This area has been
rebuilt and now features a bathroom—with a door. Trot Nixon (right)
has made the adjustment.

the idea, it was received as something of a joke. Sure. Fans on top of the Wall. Why not a glass Monster with fans inside?

"I remember John [Henry] suggesting it the first time we walked around the park after he bought the team," said Smith. "We were way out in right field, by the bullpens, and he looked over there and said, 'What about putting seats up there on top of the Wall?'"

Smith made it happen. The Henrytown project had fulfilled the promise that "people will come" while demonstrating that the new team could make significant, profitable changes without offending the purists or transforming vaunted Fenway into a honky-tonk amusement park.

The Monster Seats were a smash: they became the most coveted ducats in Major League Baseball. Stephen King wanted to sit there. Ben Affleck wanted to sit there. Local television legend Bob Lobel took to doing his live sportscast from the Monster Seats while line drives screeched toward the back of his head. Fans brought their mitts and harvested batting practice homers. It was the place to be in Boston, and we all wondered why nobody thought to do it before. And as with Henrytown, the Sox did a masterful job of making the new blend with the old. After a few days, it felt as though the Monster Seats had been there all along. In 2006 they were going for $110 (front row) and $90 (second and third rows) per game, with prices of $130 and $110 for Yankee games.

"Every suggestion, every study, every Q & A that was done with the public to ask about ways to improve Fenway Park included some idea about seats on, in, or around the Green Monster," said Smith. "So as sacred as it is—even with the screen and the divots—all that was so much part of Fenway lore, but so many fans commented on the idea. So I don't want to pretend it was novel. I think what the architectural firm brought to it was a wonderful, refined idea of how to put seats up there in a way that didn't overpower the Green Monster. And we wanted to make the seats special even after the novelty of the seats wore off."

At this point, there was no stopping Smith and friends. Henrytown was expanded in the areas on the far sides of both dugouts, gobbling up yet more of that precious foul territory. Two new rows were added in front of the backstop. Advertising panels and a new, manual, out-of-town scoreboard were added to the Wall. The Sox announced the formation of a Legends Suite, where groups of fans could pay to schmooze with Jim Lonborg, Freddie Lynn, Luis Tiant, or other Sox old-timers. This gave the owners a chance to both honor tradition and rake in more dough. Fenway was an old-fashioned giant green cash register.

In July 2003 the "Big Concourse" in right field was unveiled. Walls had been blown away and food preparation areas moved, and suddenly there was a spacious pavilion with picnic tables, new concessions and restrooms, and a customer service booth. It was truly an alternate universe to fans who'd been coming to cramped Fenway for decades.

Covering all their bases, the new owners pledged loyalty to Mayor Menino. The mayor had been marginalized by the old regime and downright insulted by Patriots owners Bob and Jonathan Kraft. Henry and Lucchino understood their suspect status as "outsiders" (many Boston media members had lobbied vigorously for the bid of local businessmen Joe O'Donnell and Steve Karp) and planned to overcome this hurdle by consulting Menino on everything short of player personnel moves. The Sox made the mayor feel involved and included (did Grady Little's lineup card get okayed by City Hall before it went up on the dugout wall?), and they were rewarded tenfold. Parking meters around the ballpark suddenly had special game day rules. The Sox took over Van Ness Street to help

with their parking needs on game day. And in September 2003 they were allowed to close off Yawkey Way before and after games. With this expanded footprint, the owners changed the Fenway experience dramatically, inviting and encouraging fans to come early and stay late. Yawkey Way was a carnival of beer, brat, jugglers, and sideshows before every game. The beloved Twins Souvenir Shop, a private (competing) business that had feuded with Harrington's people, was suddenly folded into the ballpark on game days.

Not accidentally, the whole thing was downright Camdenesque.

Next came the E Street Shuffle, Fenway as Fillmore East. Breaking decades of stodgy tradition, the Red Sox allowed Bruce Springsteen to hold two shows at Fenway in September 2003. The shows were a rousing success, and the Henry group was applauded for bringing other forms of entertainment to Boston's emerging tourist attraction. The Boss pledged to lift the Curse of the Bambino while he played on the Fenway lawn, but a month later the 2003 Red Sox season ended in painful, almost ghoulish fashion as Grady froze and Pedro Martinez gave up a 5–2 lead in the eighth inning of the seventh game of the American League Championship Series. Aaron Boone's walkoff winner sent the Sox into a winter of despair, but it also gave construction crews more time to begin the next project: a right field roof pavilion.

The following April, the Sox pulled the curtain on the new seats atop the facade where the Jimmy Fund sign stood for more than four decades. Jimmy was coldly replaced by Budweiser (ca-ching) on Opening Day, but the Sox tried to make up for it by plastering a Jimmy Fund message on the Green Monster.

Another Jimmy came to Fenway during that magical summer of 2004. Jimmy Buffett and the Coral Reefer Band stood where the Boss had played, and Mr. Margaritaville proved to be better luck than Springsteen as the Red Sox went on to win their first World Series since 1918. The new, improved Fenway was suddenly the home of the World Champions for the first time since Babe Ruth commuted to Fenway from his Dutton Road home in Sudbury, Massachusetts.

The championship was the result of some improve-

ments fans don't see. The beloved bowling alley, for example, was gutted and replaced with office space for general manager Theo Epstein and his minions. In effort to make life more comfortable for the ballplayers, the Sox also created a new players lounge and a room for their families. Down in right field, the stadium walls were blown out and modern concession areas were built. Food trucks no longer had to come into the park on a daily basis, and this made life better for fans out in the streets.

When the World Champs reported to Fenway for Opening Day 2005, they were rewarded with more amenities. There was a new batting cage next to the tunnel that connects the dugout to the clubhouse. The Scott Hatteberg memorial public urinal was replaced by a full-size, private bathroom—with a door and everything. There was a new weight training facility and a new dressing room for the umpires. Above the old bowling alley, fans poured into Game On, a spanking-new restaurant that featured plasma TVs, top-shelf liquors, and pricey hamburgers.

Later that year it was the Rolling Stones' turn to play Fenway: they destroyed the outfield grass with the largest stage in the history of concerts—a platform that approximated the size of Terminal A at Logan airport. More than four thousand square feet of outfield sod had to be replaced, but Johnny Damon was okay with the new turf once he learned that Mick Jagger had borrowed his locker before the shows.

There was no stopping it. At the end of the summer of 2005, the Sox opened the Nation's Nest, ten barstools to the left of the Monster seats. Sox fans entered lotteries for a chance to buy seats that would have served as standing room or obstructed view in most ballparks.

In the ensuing winter in which the Sox would lose Theo Epstein (he came back), Johnny Damon, Kevin Millar, and Bill Mueller, the ballpark was dramatically improved. Within hours of the final out of the 2005 season, a 5–3 Game 3 playoff loss to the White Sox, construction crews started tearing up the 406 Club behind home plate (this early elimination from the 2005 playoffs gave crews an extra three weeks to prepare for the next Opening Day). Select fans were allowed to throw cement baseballs at the stubborn glass that had insulated thousands of wealthy fans for more than a decade. In place of the 406 Club, the Sox built an open area known as the EMC Club, a section with $275 heated seats. Fans in the new seats could take advantage of waiter service, private dining rooms, a conference center, and a concierge dedicated to helping club members get tickets to ballparks across America. In addition, the Sox built a pavilion level, replacing the roof box seats and increasing Fenway's capacity from 36,298 to 38,805. The massive project represented the most extensive Fenway renovations in six decades.

The pavilion areas opened to rave reviews on April 11, 2006. Before the game, fans sat in a restaurant behind the new seats and feasted on sesame-seed tuna (pan-seared with a roasted tomato and ginger sauce) and sipped white wine. During the game, waiters served them in their cushioned, heated seats. Among other menu items at the EMC Club were Maryland-style crabcakes, filet mignon with béarnaise sauce, and crème brûlée served with a tuile cookie. It was a long way from Fenway Franks boiled in murky waters. After the home opener, Sox captain Jason Varitek said the open area behind the plate made the game louder for the ballplayers.

An enthused Henry e-mailed Lucchino and Smith: "Ideas are one thing. Execution is quite another. I could not be more thrilled with what you have accomplished this off-season. The results are simply spectacular. Larry, you and your team have transformed this grand, historic baseball park in disrepair into the greatest ballpark in America. Fifty years from now people will look back and say, 'Do you know, a lot of people wanted to tear this park down half a century ago. Can you believe that?' You are truly dream-makers of the highest order."

"Fenway was never frozen under glass," said Smith. "It's not like renovating the Capitol building, which has been special forever. Fenway constantly went through changes. We've tried to understand the place and the history. But some of what allows us to save Fenway is this moment in time. When we came along there had been fifteen years of trying to get a new ballpark. And then there was the aspect of where baseball was going. Fenway managed to survive the multipurpose-stadium era. It appeared to be a candidate for demolition during the retropark craze. Those parks started in the 50,000-seat range but gradually got smaller. So in those years, the industry standard was shrinking, and by 2002, the 36,000 seats didn't seem that far off from the 40,000 seats that teams were aiming for. Also, we haven't had to use traditional sports architects. Fenway has more in common with industrial warehouse buildings than it does with most stadiums today, so we've benefited from bringing in talent (D'Agostine, Izzo & Quirk) that's more sensitive to historic buildings and the way people use those buildings."

Future plans call for continued off-season renovations until the "new" old Fenway is complete—just in time for its 100th birthday in April 2012. Fenway will become the first ballpark to celebrate a full century of major league baseball. The National Parks Service, the Massachusetts Historic Commission, and the Boston Landmarks Commission will review all proposed changes.

The poles will remain.

"Those columns are your friends," said Smith. "There's no other way to have the seats upstairs as close and as low as they are at Fenway Park."

And it'll still be dark when you walk through the concourse—that way your son or daughter will get the same thrill you had when they walk up a ramp and through a portal into Fenway for the first time.

It still has to be Fenway Park.

The ballpark is the star. In the age of Tris Speaker and Babe Ruth,

the era of Jimmie Foxx and Ted Williams,

through the empty-seat epoch of Don Buddin and Willie Tasby,

and into the decades of Carl Yastrzemski and Jim Rice,

the ballpark is the star.

— MARTIN F. NOLAN

I think walking up to Fenway is thrilling.

The approach to it. The smells. You go to Fenway and you revert to your childhood.

You go to Fenway and you think,

"Something wonderful's going to happen today."

— DAVID HALBERSTAM

How far away must one sit to be safe in this park?

I didn't even get the ball.

— Red Sox fan **JOSEPH A. BOUCHER,** who was conked in the head

by Ted Williams's 502-foot home run into the right field bleachers.

A red seat marks the spot where Boucher sat and Ted struck.

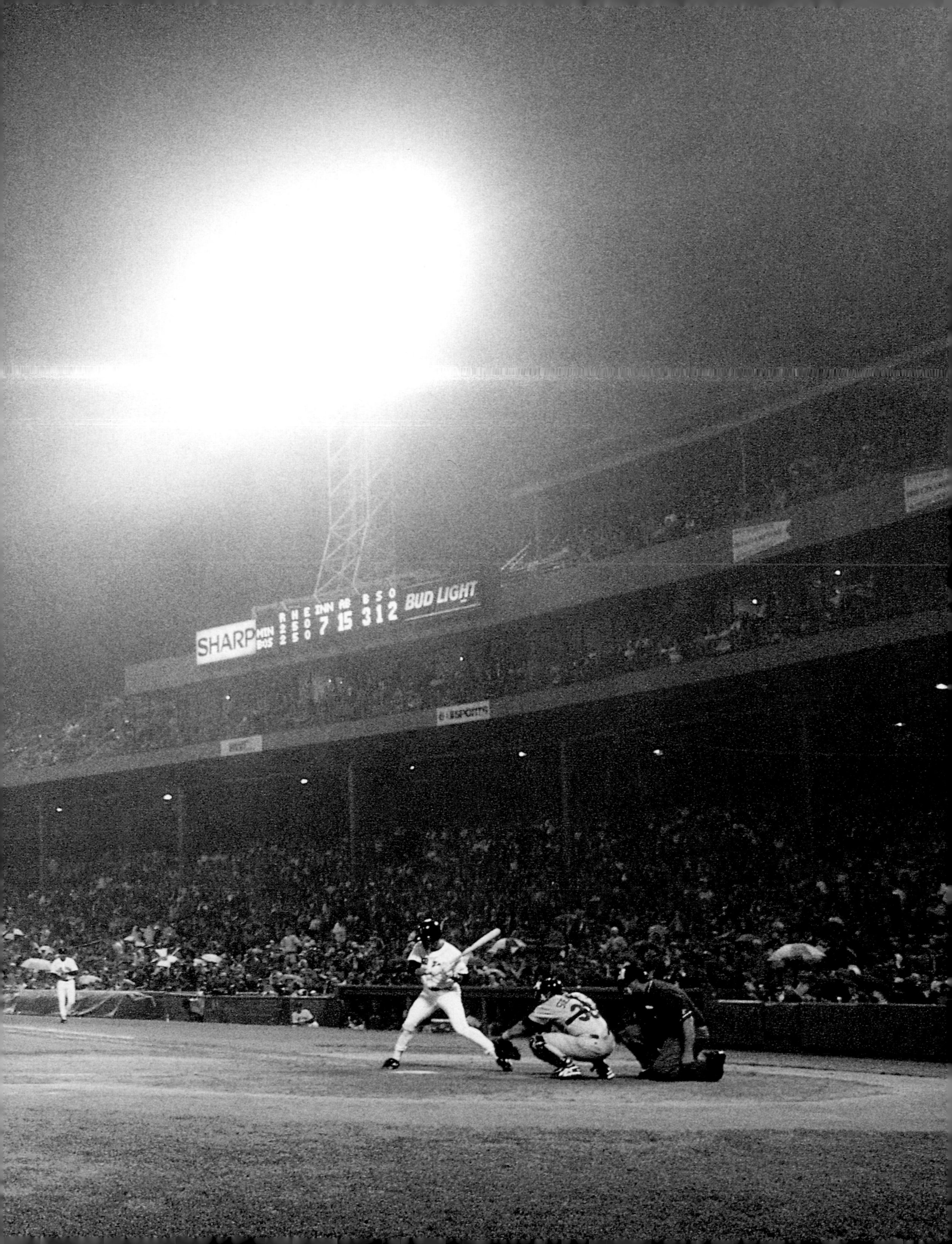
SHARP
BUD LIGHT

I take some weird comfort in the knowledge that these poles

are the same green beams that blocked the vision of my dad and his dad

when they would take the trolley in from Cambridge

to watch the Red Sox in the 1920s.

— DAN SHAUGHNESSY

Recipe for Fenway grass:

85 percent Kentucky bluegrass, 15 percent perennial ryegrass,

lots of water, lots of love, and keep the fans off the field.

— JOE MOONEY, GROUNDSKEEPER, EMERITUS

Fenway Park is a friendly neighborhood joint,

the corner bar of American sports palaces.

— DAN SHAUGHNESSY

It's like being in an English theatre.

You're right on top of the stage. So chummy.

— TIP O'NEILL

Perhaps the field should be renamed Fenway No-Park

because there is no place to beach your car.

— DAN SHAUGHNESSY

It is a New England landmark, no less so than the Bunker Hill Monument, Plymouth Rock, or Walden Pond. And when major league baseball is no longer played in Fenway Park, there is a good chance that the left field wall will be preserved, either as part of the next park or as a monument to the

first century of American League baseball in Boston.

It was built to keep baseballs in play, but its beauty is the memory of all the balls that have sailed over it. No one knows when the left field wall was first called the Green Monster, but it stands upright as the signature feature of this singular baseball park.

It is probably the Wall's appeal to young people that explains its lasting fame. A six-year-old at his or her first big league game might walk into Camden Yards in Baltimore, Jacobs Field in Cleveland, or even Yankee Stadium in the Bronx, and never remember anything specific about the park itself. But a little kid going to his or her first game in Boston is sure to remember the first breathtaking glance at the huge wall in left field. It's big and green and unlike any facade in professional sports. Children remember the Green Monster the way they remember their first look at the Grand Canyon or the Golden Gate Bridge. Size matters. The Green Monster is impossible to ignore or forget.

More than any quirky feature, the Wall has come to symbolize and encapsulate the Fenway experience. The Boston Garden had its parquet floor (which has been moved to the New Garden), Wrigley Field has ivy-covered bricks in the outfield, and Notre Dame football is played in the shadow of the Golden Dome under the watchful

eye of Touchdown Jesus, but Fenway's Wall is the most identifiable feature of any sports venue in America.

When network television cameras broadcast a Red Sox game across the country, fans in Des Moines see the Wall and instantly know that the game is being played in Boston. It's like hearing the chowder-thick accent of Ted Kennedy on a newscast. It's everything Boston.

The Wall is a larger part of Boston's baseball history than Ted Williams or Carl Yastrzemski. It is worshiped by hitters, feared by pitchers, and alternately mastered and butchered by outfielders who want to play its unconventional caroms. Managers have lost their hair trying to make the Wall work in their favor, and too many pitchers and hitters have changed their natural practices in an attempt to take advantage of what the Wall offers and denies. The Baltimore Oriole pitchers used to do an imitation of the short Sox righty Marty Pattin pitching in Fenway. The routine involved staring in for the sign from the catcher, getting the sign, then turning around to look at the Wall and shaking off the sign. Once. Twice. Three times. That was Marty Pattin, scared to pitch with the Green Monster lurking over his right shoulder.

Fenway's left field wall is 37 feet high and capped by three rows of Monster Seats, which are the hottest tickets in baseball. The Wall is 240 feet long and was originally

constructed from thirty thousand pounds of Toncan iron in 1934. Its reinforced steel and concrete foundation sinks 22 feet below the field.

Signs advertising whiskey, razor blades, and soap covered the Wall for more than ten seasons before it was painted green in 1947. Today Monster Green is a custom blend made by John Smith, a commercial painter in Wilmington, Massachusetts, who inherited the job from his father, the late Ken Smith. The initials of Thomas A. Yawkey and his wife, Jean, are set in Morse code on its

scoreboard. The Wall was rebuilt in 1976: old tin panels were replaced by a Formica-type covering that yielded more consistent caroms and less noise (the tin panels were cut into small squares and sold, the proceeds going to the Jimmy Fund). When the old wall was in place, batting practice shots in an empty Fenway produced a clang; now it's something closer to a thud.

At the foul pole, the Wall is only 309 feet and 3 inches from home plate, but for most of the century the Red Sox posted a sign that read "315." Club officials

are dreamers, and most of them played a little hardball in their day. Is there a healthy male in his twenties, thirties, or forties who doesn't believe he could stand in Fenway's batter's box and line a couple of shots off or over the Green Monster?

One of baseball's last hand-operated scoreboards is inside the Wall. There a few part-time Sox employees slide 2-pound 12-by-16-inch numbers into slots to tell fans how the Sox are doing and how things are shaping up around the American League. When there's a pennant race and fans are rooting for the Sox to overtake the Yankees, there can be quite a bit of suspense when the kids behind the green door take down a zero and show them that the Orioles have just scored six against New York in Yankee Stadium. No electronic message board can duplicate this thrill.

The Wall has no permanent bathroom, although portables have been used. It's dark, dirty, and designed for Quasimodo. Rat poison lines the floor. It's boiling in the summertime and freezing in the spring and fall. But the kids get to talk with opposing left fielders, and Ted Williams said some of his favorite Fenway memories were chats with the faceless, Oz-like men behind the scoreboard. Tours of Fenway were instituted in the 1990s, and fans are allowed to duck into the room in the Wall. Some of the graffiti are pretty rough, but if you look hard enough you may find some signatures from members of the ground crew and American League players of the last half century. Walk into this secret sanctuary and the first thing you see is the names of Wall workers Dave Savoy, Jim Reid, and Billy Fitzgerald under the heading "1961 All-Star Game." One can only presume that these three young men manned the big board for the midsummer classic during the John F. Kennedy administration.

"I worked inside the Wall for a couple of summers," recalls Joe Cochran, the equipment manager of the Red Sox. "Not every night, but enough games to know what it's like. One night it was so hot, I wound up working in just my boots and boxer shorts. There's drainpipes out there, and I used to see rats' noses poking through. We had a portable toilet, so that helped. Later, when I'd be in the dugout with the team, I'd call to the scoreboard and tell them the Yankees or Tigers just got ten runs in the

refused to allow anyone to measure the real distance, but when the *Boston Globe* snuck into Fenway and came up with the new figure, the Sox grudgingly changed the sign. Major league rules today stipulate that no fence in any new park be closer than 325 feet from home plate, but this will probably be waived if the Sox choose to duplicate the Wall in a different park. The term "grandfather clause" was invented for Fenway Park.

The Wall's massive dimensions make it appear closer than it is, and that, too, is part of its appeal. Baseball fans

Top: Scoreboard operator Chris Elias watches the action from inside the left field wall.

Above: Ancient graffiti inside the Wall commemorates Ted Williams's homers in 1951.

first inning. The poor kid would post the ten and the whole crowd would groan." In 1975, the late NBC director Harry Coyle put a camera inside the left field wall. Legend has it that a rat appeared, which froze the camera operator and resulted in the best baseball video clip of all time. The unattended camera was focused on home plate and caught Carlton Fisk waving his arms, willing his fly ball into fair territory. His drive caromed off the left field foul pole, and NBC was rewarded with a clip capturing what *TV Guide* in 1998 ranked as the greatest moment in the history of sports television.

There are plenty of other signatures inside the wall. John Stone and John Giuliotti of the ground crew signed while working the 1986 World Series. To the right of their signatures is the autograph of Jimmy Piersall, a master defensive outfielder and baserunner for the Sox in the 1950s. He became famous when his biography, *Fear Strikes Out,* was made into a major motion picture, starring Anthony Perkins, of *Psycho* fame. Piersall went from Fenway to a mental institution, but in 1957 he was idolized by the kids inside the Wall and they kept track of his home runs, both at Fenway and on the road; the evidence is still there. Other graffiti indicate that somebody inside the Wall logged the home runs hit by Ted Williams in 1951 (there were 30). Meanwhile, there are signatures from current and former big leaguers: Andy Pettitte, Troy O'Leary, Curt Schilling, Scott Kamieniecki, Darren Holmes, Chuck Crim, Chris Bosio, Chuck Knoblauch, Steve Bedrosian, Scott Erickson, and Tim Salmon. There's a message from Oil Can Boyd—"The Can"—and a marking from Boo Ferriss, 1945–50. There's even graffiti from the turbulent '60s—"Free Angela" and "Stop the War."

According to Joe Mooney, former Sox groundskeeper, the Wall is a fine conductor of heat. When Fenway was buried in snow on April Fool's Day, 1997 (while the Sox were opening the season on the West Coast), Mooney piled snow up against the Wall, claiming it melted faster that way.

In July 1998, the second year of interleague play, the Phillies veteran infielder Rex Hudler made Fenway part of his nostalgic tour. He snatched some ivy from the bricks at Wrigley Field, then went inside the Wall at Fenway and came away with a broken red light about the size of a small satellite dish. Hudler said someday he'll tell his kids that Mo Vaughn hit a screaming line drive right through the light. Hudler also used an old bolt to scratch his name inside the Wall. (The thirty-eight-year-old Hudler was released by the Phillies a day after his Fenway heist.) Several latter-day heroes signed their names when the All-Stars came back to Fenway in the summer of 1999.

For decades, the Wall has artificially inflated the numbers of Boston's right-handed batters and encouraged the Red Sox to field a team of slow, big-swinging, righty sluggers. Assembling this kind of team has been done at the expense of speed and fundamentals. The Wall teaches a manager to eschew the bunt, forget the hit-and-run, and wait for the game-breaking, 3-run homer. It has scared generations of left-handed pitchers, and rare is the southpaw who will pitch inside at Fenway (the last Red Sox lefty to win 20 games was Mel Parnell, in 1953). The Wall has encouraged the Red Sox to design teams that have trouble winning away games; historically, the Sox have been embarrassed on the artificial turf of Kansas City and also in Yankee Stadium, where left field is several acres larger than in Boston. The 1949 Red Sox went 61–16 at home but only 35–42 on the road, losing the American League pennant in New York when they dropped the final two games of the season.

Many Sox fans believe that the Wall was the undoing of George Scott in 1968. Scott hit .303 during the Impossible Dream season of 1967 but a year later dropped to .171, with 3 homers. Ask Sal Bando what it did to him during the 1975 ALCS. In the second game of the playoffs, at Fenway, Bando hit four shots off the Wall; at least a couple of them would have been homers in most other ballparks. Bando's harvest was 2 singles and 2 doubles.

American League outfielders have been confounded by the Wall for more than seventy years. There can be little doubt that Carl Yastrzemski was the master of Wall-ball defense. An infielder as a collegian at Notre Dame, Yastrzemski had the coordination, the instincts, and the work ethic to make the Wall work for him. He was among the American League's outfield assist leaders annually until baserunners learned to stop going for two when they clanged one off the Wall. Yaz could decoy better than any outfielder and routinely pretended he was ready to catch a ball that he knew was going to carom off the Wall. Sometimes this would make runners slow down or stop altogether. Yaz had another Wall habit that annoyed some Boston pitchers. When a slugger unloaded on a meatball from a Sox hurler, Yaz would sometimes stand motionless, hands on hips, staring forward as the ball sailed over his head, over the screen, and out toward the Mass. Turnpike. He didn't want to give the hitter the satisfaction of turning around, and sometimes it was a message to a Boston pitcher who may have thrown the wrong pitch to the wrong guy.

"I knew when the ball was going out," said Yastrzemski. "It was something I worked into the decoy. But it used to tick the pitchers off. Bill Monbouquette used to say, 'Can't you at least make it look like you can catch it?' Meanwhile, the ball would be on its way over the fence to a spot three-quarters of the way out to the railroad tracks."

Jim Rice followed Yaz to the left field pasture in 1975 and suffered from comparisons with the Hall of Famer. Rice never got better than average defensively, but he did learn the Wall and its caroms, which give visiting outfielders fits. Earl Weaver, the former Oriole manager, still laughs at the thought of Don Baylor trying to play the Wall when the O's came to Boston. Baylor once got tangled up in the left field corner, trying to corral a ball that was rattling around the doorway in the corner and men in the Oriole dugout (which has no view of the corner) wondered what had happened as they watched the Red Sox runners going around the bases. It was one of those "only in Fenway" moments.

The Wall has a ladder that enabled the ground crew to pluck home run balls from the screen above in the old days. It's the only fair-territory ladder in the majors. One night in the '50s, Ted Williams and Jimmy Piersall converged under a fly ball in left center. To their surprise, the ball hit the ladder and ricocheted toward center, allowing Jim Lemon to circle the bases for an inside-the-park homer. Another one of those moments came in 1963 when the Sox stonefinger slugger Dick Stuart—a man with all the speed of an ox—hit an inside-the-park home run in Fenway. His towering fly to left center hit the lad-

der, then bounced off the head of the Cleveland center fielder, Vic Davalillo, and rolled to the left field corner. By the time Davalillo ran down the ball, Stuart had chugged around the bases.

The Wall has made heroes out of hitters like Walt Dropo, Stuart, Tony Conigliaro, Rico Petrocelli, George Scott, Ken Harrelson, Rice, Butch Hobson, Tony Perez, Tony Armas, and Dwight Evans. It has helped the Red Sox draw fans and boast of home run champions. It has created excitement and memories, but it has hurt the Red Sox by artificially inflating the abilities of the ball club. It has tipped the scales of baseball's balance, distorting the product and creating advantages and disadvantages that are patently unfair. Never was this more obvious than on the afternoon of October 2, 1978, when Bucky Dent hit a weak pop-up that plopped into the screen and forever changed the course of Red Sox history.

Dent's home run beat the Red Sox in the infamous one-game playoff of 1978, denying the best Boston team of the last half century its chance to compete in the postseason. It's a cruel joke that a sawed-off shortstop representing the New York Yankees would be the one to use the Wall like no other player in baseball history.

Fenway Park was a home of champions in its earliest days. The 1912 Red Sox christened it with a World Series victory, and the Sox won the World Series again in 1915, 1916, and 1918. Even the Boston Braves used Fenway for their Series sweep of Philadelphia in 1914.

But Fenway and the World Series were strangers for most of the next eighty-six years. The Fall Classic visited Jersey Street–Yawkey Way four times between 1918 and 2004, and each time the Red Sox lost the Series in a crushing seventh game. Two of those Game Seven defeats (1967 and 1975) were played on the Fenway lawn. It was presidential speechwriter Richard Goodwin who in 1999 pointed out, "It hasn't exactly been a good luck charm."

And then everything changed in 2004, creating what owner John Henry called "an alternative universe."

Indeed. Two thousand and four was the year when pigs flew, cows jumped over a giant red moon in the late October sky, and the Red Sox finally won another World Series.

Fenway's role in the magical season of 2004 was significant, but sadly, the clinching moments played out on stages in New York and St. Louis. The Red Sox won the American League pennant on Wednesday night, October 20, beating the Yankees at Yankee Stadium, 10–3. For the Red Sox players, front office personnel, and the few fans who made the trip, there was no sweeter moment than seeing the Sox spraying champagne on the Yankee Stadium infield after so many decades of torture at the hands of the Pinstripe Gang. In that sense, winning on the road was better than winning at Fenway.

The World Series, however, was another matter. The Series opened in Fenway Park because the American League had thrashed National League starter Roger Clemens en route to a 9–4 victory in the 2004 All-Star Game in Houston. This gave the Red Sox Games 1 and 2, plus 6 and 7 if necessary. The middle three games were slated for St. Louis. In most years, this format would have put the Red Sox at home for the clinching game of the World Series, but the Sox were on a redoubtable roll at

the end of 2004, and there would be no Game 5, 6, or 7. They swept the Cardinals in four and thus found themselves more than a thousand miles southwest of Fenway when Keith Foulke flipped an Edgar Renteria grounder to Doug Mientkiewicz for the final out of the World Series.

But Fenway was good to the new champs. The curse-busting Sox went 55-26 at home during the regular season and 5-2 at Fenway in the stardust-sprinkled run through the playoffs. It was in the summer of 2004 that traditional songs like "Sweet Caroline," "Dirty Water," and "Tessie" took on new life at the ancient yard.

And there were Fenway moments that shall forever be discussed when Sox fans gather to discuss that championship season. First and foremost, during the regular season, there was the infamous rain-delayed, fight-filled, ejection-laden, 11–10 Red Sox walkoff victory over the hated Yankees on July 24. This was the game that turned around the Red Sox season, and it came on a rainy Fenway Saturday when most of the Yankees wanted to

pack up and go back to their hotel. Instead, the game was played, and the signature moment of the 2004 season came when Jason Varitek smashed his catcher's mitt into the handsome face of Alex Rodriguez in the third inning, when the Sox trailed, 3–0. The brawl awakened the Red Sox, who eventually won the game on a Bill Mueller two-run homer off Mariano Rivera in the bottom of the ninth. Fenway may have never been louder.

The Sox were in Tampa when they clinched a spot in the playoffs, and as we said, they were in New York and St. Louis for their final two champagne celebrations. The only clinch party at Fenway that year came on the night of October 8, when David Ortiz (who else?) crushed a two-out, two-run homer into the Monster Seats in the bottom of the tenth. Señor October's blast came at 8:21 P.M., triggering one of the most electrifying moments in the history of a ballpark that's almost older than household electricity.

The Red Sox and Yankees played the middle three of

the American League Championship Series at Fenway, and few will forget what happened in the first one. It was Saturday, October 16, and the Yankees embarrassed six Boston pitchers, laughing their way to a 19–8 victory in 4 hours and 20 minutes of Hub humiliation. But the Sox rebounded in their Back Bay basilica. Game 4 featured Dave Roberts's stolen-base-for-the-ages, and Big Papi won it in the bottom of the twelfth with yet another walkoff home run. The game ended at 1:22 A.M. on the morning of October 18, and 15 hours and 49 minutes after Ortiz circled the bases, Fenway was full again for Pedro Martinez's first pitch to Derek Jeter in Game 5. In the ninth inning, Fenway's odd right field wall—down past the Pesky pole—figured in a ground-rule double, which kept the Yankees off the scoreboard and enabled the Sox to win again, this time in the bottom of the fourteenth, again on a walkoff hit by Ortiz. The Sox carried their momentum to New York and won two more times to clinch the American League pennant.

The World Series at Fenway was almost anticlimactic. And it's a shame that the 2004 Red Sox could not celebrate the end of eighty-six years of frustration at home. Mark Bellhorn's eighth-inning, two-run homer off Pesky's pole won Game 1, 11–9, and Curt Schilling brought back the bloody sock to win the second game, 6–2, at Fenway.

But that was the last baseball played at Fenway in 2004. The Steamroller Sox swept two more games, becoming the first team in major league history to win eight consecutive postseason games in a single year. The streak started in Fenway Park with Dave Roberts's stolen base against the Yankees, and when the Sox finally won in St. Louis, New England fans streamed toward Fenway in the early morning hours. They were pilgrims, trekking to the sacred place where major league baseball has been played and celebrated for almost a hundred years. Finally, Fenway Park was again home to the champions of baseball.

I'll never forgive myself or my team.

As good as we were, there's no way

we should have lost

four games in a row

to anyone.

— ALEX RODRIGUEZ

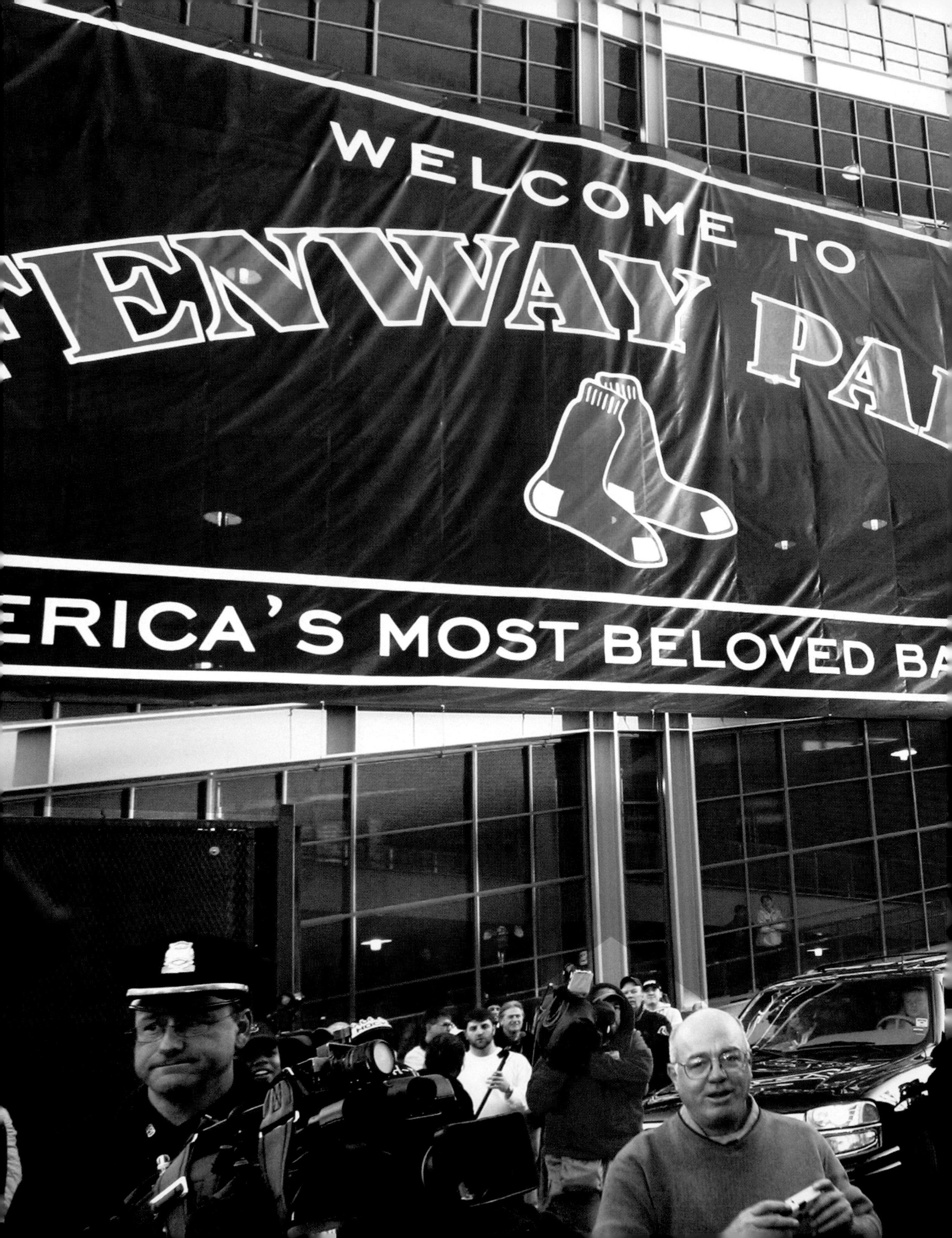
WELCOME TO
ENWAY PA
ERICA'S MOST BELOVED BA

It gave us a collective, cathartic exhale.

The region dumped all its collective baggage at once.

— THEO EPSTEIN

David Halberstam

David Halberstam is a Pulitzer Prize–winning author and historian.

I HAD A SPLIT CHILDHOOD. I WENT TO MY FIRST game at Yankee Stadium with my father, and he told me to watch the way the great DiMaggio rounded second base. But I had an uncle in Boston named Harry Levy. He cofounded a store in Boston, a wholesale paint store, and he prospered and bought season tickets to the Red Sox games. I remember hearing this during the war, and the idea that anybody in our family would have season tickets was amazing. In '46 he took me to Fenway, and we sat about five rows behind the first base dugout. That was the Red Sox team with Rudy York, Johnny Pesky, Bobby Doerr, and Birdie Tebbetts. I was twelve. It was amazing. You could really see their faces. Rudy York's face was really red. When I go to Fenway now, I can still see the twelve-year-old boy and I can hear my uncle Harry saying, "They're such fine-looking young men." And later in my life I met them and they were such fine men. I don't think I've ever met a better human being in my life than Bobby Doerr.

At that age, you don't know what it is you like about a ballpark. Now I know that what I saw was intimacy. You could see them. You felt connected. And it wasn't just that these seats were very good. Almost anywhere in Fenway you feel connected. There are no distant seats. There really is a feeling of connection and intimacy.

As I grow older, I think of Fenway, and I think of everybody wearing a jacket, a tie, a boater, and maybe Babe Ruth is going to pitch against Smokey Joe Wood. You really think that it goes back in time. I really like the sense of connection in life. I want my daughter to grow up valuing the things I value. I'd love for her in forty or fifty years to fish from Nantucket. I would be thrilled if she lived in the same house. And I love the idea of Fenway, of a connection to the past. When you go there, you're watching where people watched Babe Ruth pitch, where DiMaggio and Williams had their epic battles. It's where Jimmy Foxx and Ellis Kinder and Mel Parnell had their great seasons. I like it when the past reverberates in our lives. Our daughter went to a great boarding school, and there's nothing more thrilling to me than the Groton chapel. Franklin Roosevelt, Sixth Form (senior class) of 1900. President of the United States, 1933–45. Dean Acheson—Sixth Form of whatever it is—1911, then secretary of state of the United States. Things like that are thrilling to me.

My father introduced me to baseball, so it gives me a great sense of connection. I love Fenway. Even the things that are wrong with it have a quality of humanity. There's a danger in this society of inhumanity, of building parks that are not for fans but are really for tax writeoffs. For basketball, I liked Chicago Stadium better than the United Center. I don't think the New Garden is any better than the old Boston Garden. I wouldn't want to go to the United Center and have my knees cramped up, but I think it's part of the bargain at a place like Fenway Park. Fenway is very democratic. I don't think the new parks are as democratic because of the price of the ticket. That changes the new parks and arenas. I know the owners have a dilemma, but blue-collar families now can only go once or twice a year.

I didn't go to Fenway games when I was at Harvard. After my childhood experience, I started going again with pals in the 1980s. I went with my friends at the *Globe*. Then I wrote a piece on the Opening Day in 1989 or 1990. It was the first time I had written on deadline in a while. Billy Cleary of Harvard threw out the first ball.

There are certain new things in the world that aren't an improvement. A nice ballpark is a really wonderful thing. And it's so nice to be able to walk to it or take a trolley. I think walking up to Fenway is thrilling. The approach to it. The smells. You go to Fenway and you revert to your childhood. It has a kind of magical quality rather than a functional quality that one generally associates with childhood and the unknown. You go to Fenway and you think, "Something wonderful's going to happen today." Now we're older and you take things in stride, but when you are a kid and you grow up without a lot of money, there's a magical quality to going to a ballpark like Fenway. We didn't have television then, so you didn't take it for granted.

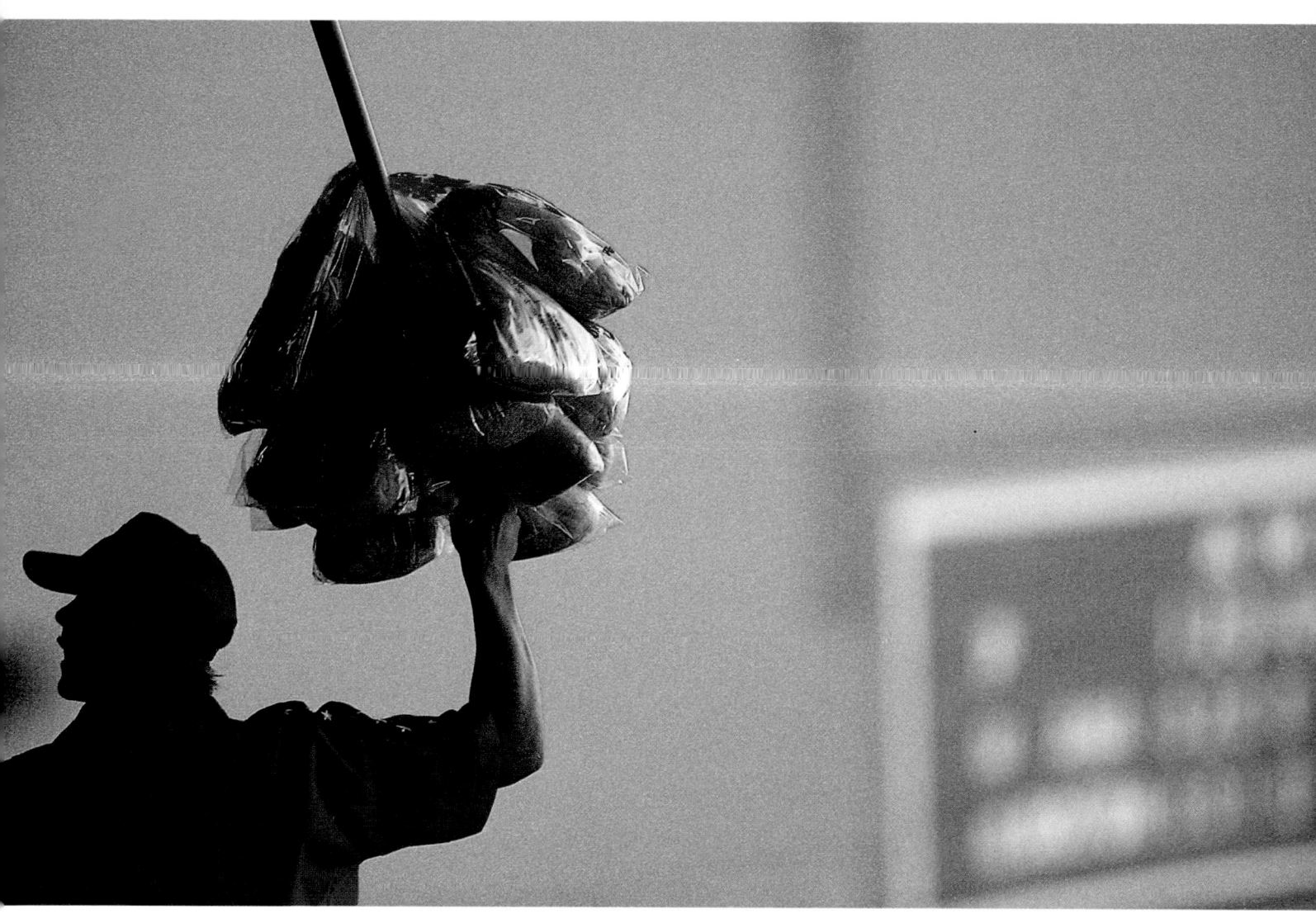

I believe that these temples are our secular cathedrals,

and they tell us as much about what we care about as anything in our environment.

— KEN BURNS

> For years, you had to have a couple of beers in you before you'd eat a hot dog because the hot dogs came out of this murky water that looked like something from the Okefenokee Swamp.
>
> — STEPHEN KING

Stephen King

Stephen King, the best-selling author, is a Red Sox season ticket holder.

DOESN'T EVERYBODY REMEMBER THEIR FIRST time at Fenway? I was twelve years old. We went down from Maine with my cousin, who had his driver's license. It was a gray day. The Red Sox were playing the Tigers. It was either 1959 or '60. Ted Williams was still playing, and Al Kaline was playing for the Tigers. The game was an official game, but it was called after six innings because of rain. Detroit won, and I think Norm Cash hit a home run. What I remember was coming up the runway and out into the park and just being flattened by the beauty of it, by the green. And the day was gray, but the grass was the greenest green I'd ever seen—and I was a country boy.

We sat on the third base side, under the overhang, up pretty high. I didn't have an affinity for Ted at the time because my uncle hated him. My uncle was the kind of guy who'd get two or three beers in him and start saying, "That goddamned Williams. He don't try worth a darn." He was a real Red Sox fan.

Between the ages of twelve and twenty, I probably saw them once a year, and I used to brag because except for that first game—and I don't think it should really count because it didn't go nine—I never saw them lose. I've often thought that I would like to write a story or even a novel where some columnist finds this old guy who's never seen the Red Sox lose. He's been to a lot of games, and they find out that when they bring this guy into the park, they always win, so they prop him up and get to the World Series, and the guy has a couple of strokes and a heart attack and they're still bringing him in. Of course, the kicker is, he dies before the seventh game.

In college, I went to Fenway more. I had an old Ford station wagon, and my friend, who was a real fan, and I would hop into that and make the six-hour drive from the University of Maine to Fenway. It's a hike, but we didn't mind. I didn't become a regular customer until I got enough money to be able to do it. I became a season ticket holder in 1986. I started to do that because I was going down a lot and I was scrounging for tickets. My first season tickets were on the first base line, and we were there for a while. My clearest memory comes from my youngest son, Owen, who's now almost thirty. In '86 he was nine, and he came down for the third game of the World Series on a school night. Oil Can Boyd pitched and we lost the game. Owen was a huge Red Sox fan and he was up late and it had been a stressful day, and as we left the ballpark he started to cry, and I said, "Now you're a Red Sox fan." We joke about it because we have to joke about it, but it hurts and you learn to live with that. I can remember walking up that ramp and him crying. You can't help it. It's not like you're being cruel to the kid, he's a New Englander. He's in New York now, but he still calls up every night and asks, "What's the score?"

In '78, I watched the Red Sox–Yankees playoff game on TV. I canceled classes that year. It's the only time I ever did that. Through hangovers, sexual obsessions, and everything else, that was the one time I canceled anything.

I love Fenway. I love it in spite of the things about it that I hate. It's dirty, it's crumbly. For years, you had to have a couple of beers in you before you'd eat a hot dog because the hot dogs came out of this murky water that looked like something from the Okefenokee Swamp. And you could never get anything to put on the hot dogs. I'd ask if they had any catsup and the guy would say, "We got mustard on the post." And he's giving you that look, that Boston look. And if you like the mustard, that's good. If you don't, too bad. I've sat behind a pole. There was a big game in '85 when I had to do that, and that's when I decided to get season tickets.

The park doesn't work anymore. My seats now are down beyond third base, and there are fans behind the aisle and they lose everything every time someone passes by. If you want a beer, you have to go out and get it. You can't sit in the stands and get a beer. That means you have to be dedicated to the idea of that beer. You have to get up and actually stir around a little bit. People don't complain, but part of that is that people feel they are part of history when they come to the park.

But I love the people who've been there over the years. You get to know the people who are regulars, and they get to know you. I like the old guys that wipe off your seat. They seem like they were there when the club came in. I love all the little nooks and crannies and places to go—the idea that there's a scoreboard and somebody's behind it, putting up numbers. There's no place like it, and it's ours.

With the team, we've had good days and bad days, and we've had teams where the wheels kind of fell off. But we do have the park. I have memories of Wes Gardner pitching a 1–0 shutout and the full moon rising up over the park and Bob Stanley popping out of the stands and grabbing those beach balls and popping them. You can't trade that stuff. When you're younger you think it's nothing and then later on you realize it's a lot.

I think it's easier to be a traditionalist when you are young. If they move on, I'll know I had it with my kids. It's like players move on. You try to tell people now that there was this guy, Joe Foy, who was our Troy O'Leary, and they don't know what you're talking about. I've got this ace-in-the-hole in the back of my mind that they will never move because Boston is so goddamned corrupt that it'll be forty or fifty years before they grease enough palms. And furthermore, even once they get going, they will stretch the job out. When they open the new stadium, I'll go in my wheelchair and you can go in your walker. I love Fenway.

James Taylor

James Taylor is a Grammy Award–winning singer and songwriter and a member of the Rock and Roll Hall of Fame.

I WENT WITH MY DAD WHEN I WAS A KID, BUT I DON'T remember it. I was born in 1948 and we left Boston in 1951, and it was during that period when he says he took my older brother and me. We moved to North Carolina, and my memories of baseball are college games and minor league fields. I didn't really get back to Boston until I moved to Martha's Vineyard in the early '80s. I didn't come back to Fenway until I went with my dad again in the mid-1980s. He had a couple of boys in Little League with his second wife, Sue, and they would go occasionally to Fenway and I accompanied them on one of those trips.

It felt like it was from another time, that it belonged to a different kind of baseball and a different sensibility and, really, a different America than what I had come to think of as a modern stadium. It just had a personability about it, a genteelness about it. That was my impression. I'm not saying that Boston fans are genteel. You look at old pictures of the park, and everybody's got a suit on and a derby hat. That's probably as rowdy a crowd as it is today. They just look that way because it's an old black-and-white picture.

It's hell to perform there. It's great, but when you sing for a living, you're used to being behind the sound system.

So you get some talk back from the house. But when the speakers are 150 yards away and blasting back at you with that kind of second and a half delay, it's a real challenge to sing with that. Some people do it better than others. It's made a lot easier for me with ear monitors. You can focus on what you're doing in real time rather than what you did a second and a half ago. I've performed there three times and did a sound check each time. Once was on Patriots Day, once before the second game of the 2004 World Series—both of those were the national anthem. Then I performed "America the Beautiful" before Opening Day in 2005, when they handed out the championship rings.

Playing at Fenway feels like a hometown crowd. There's an element to it for me that's like playing at the Tweeter Center or Tanglewood or up at Manchester, New Hampshire. It feels like a hometown, New England crowd. The other thing about it is that you really are part of the action. When you're doing the anthem, it's not like everybody's focused on you and they come there to see you. They come there to see a ball game, and that's just one of the fixtures there.

The World Series game was amazing. After that impossible miracle of winning four straight against the Yankees, it was almost like being in an altered state. At that point, I did feel a sense of invincibility about the Sox. Schilling's heroic effort, struggling forth with wounds, it was really an amazing thing. I was so impressed with Curt Schilling. I got pissed off at him for the political actions later on, but the fact remains that he's a real hero for doing that.

I have not taken my boys to Fenway yet. They were a little young last year. They're five now, and they came by when I did "America the Beautiful" but didn't really sit in the stands. They'd just turned four. One of the reasons I've been spending so much time at Fenway recently is because I like to see my wife every once in a while. I'm basically a baseball widower. Kim is the mover and shaker who got me the opportunity to play the anthem there. I worked on it. Given my particular style, it was harder to work up a concise arrangement that's bulletproof. That took some doing. There's nothing like the reality of the Fenway crowd staring you in the face to focus your mind.

Doris Kearns Goodwin

Doris Kearns Goodwin is a Pulitzer Prize–winning author, a historian, and a Red Sox season ticket holder.

I FELL IN LOVE WITH FENWAY PARK BEFORE I FELL in love with the Red Sox. I came to Boston in the fall of '64 for graduate school at Harvard, but I didn't go to Fenway until the next summer. The first time I went to Fenway Park was actually the first time I'd been to a baseball game since the Dodgers left Brooklyn [1957]. I just lost any caring about baseball once the Dodgers left Brooklyn. My father had made the transition to the Mets, but I couldn't make any transition. So really, baseball had left my life. It was partly also my age, I suppose. It was during that time when I graduated from high school and then college. But somehow, that very first time I went to Fenway Park—a boyfriend took me and it was a beautiful summer night, probably in June—and somehow all the memories of Ebbetts Field came back. It was the same kind of park, small and overcrowded, and there were lots of people there even though the Red Sox weren't doing well then. All the peculiar characteristics of the park brought back memories of Ebbetts Field. Probably most important, the fans were so close to the field—yelling and screaming and knowing what was going on—and that was so reminiscent of the Brooklyn Dodgers. So my return to baseball, and the beginning of what has now been another three decades of obsession, started with that first night at Fenway Park.

I know where I sat that night, and it's still my favorite place. We somehow had lower box seats between home and first. Later, when my husband and I got our first season tickets in 1976, they were in that same area. Now we've been upgraded to the area below the walkway aisle, but we're between home and third base, and I don't feel the same familiarity. I still miss that other place.

We started taking our boys when they were about three or four. We didn't stay for the whole game. They loved to go for the hot dogs and all the food. We gradually worked them into it, and by '86 they were full-fledged fans. The fact that it was small meant that they felt a mastery of it even as little kids. I can still remember that feeling when you walk down the ramp when you first come in and turn right, and they knew exactly where to run to go to our seats. I suppose you could learn that in a big Astrodome, but not with the same sense of comfort. When they got a little older, I felt comfortable letting them go to get a snack by themselves. You knew they'd find their way back. And there was a wonderful guy in the information booth. Al. He's a terrific fellow. He's been there forever. He used to be an usher and we only had three seats in '86, and he let Joey, who was only nine, sneak in and sit on our laps during the World Series. There was a specialness in that for the boys. They would come in and high-five him. Even now they go to talk to him, and I think that creates part of the familiarity of a small park and the people who've been there for a long time that I don't think would be the same in a larger place.

Fenway becomes like a piece of furniture in your household. It's as if you've got a couch that may be a little bit old and torn in places, but it's comfortable and familiar, and it's got a lot of memories.

> Fenway becomes like a piece of furniture in your household.
>
> It's as if you've got a couch that may be a little bit old and torn in places, but
>
> it's comfortable and familiar, and it's got a lot of memories.
>
> — DORIS KEARNS GOODWIN

Yo-Yo Ma

Yo-Yo Ma is a world-renowned cellist and one of the best-selling classical recording artists.

THE FIRST TIME I CAME HERE WAS SOMETIME IN the 1990s. We got the tickets at one of the school events at Buckingham, Browne & Nichols, and we ended up in the bleachers and had a wonderful time. The only other park I had been in was the old Comiskey Park. I remember feeling how much more intimate Fenway was than Comiskey Park.

I always look at gatherings for what the feeling is. What the feel is of the space that actually contributes to the reception of the activity. My sense of the space at Fenway is that it really is there both for the players as well as for the public. There's such an incredible connection. I remember my daughter Emily calling me from Fenway when she went to her first game about two years ago. She was already a rabid fan, and when she called me from the game, she was almost trembling with excitement. You would feel that electricity in the air. It's great to be able to come to Fenway with my daughter. I think you can count us as lifers. And in the summer of 2006 she got her favorite job ever—she got to work at Fenway. Seventy-hour weeks, and she loved it.

I know these days a lot of the major league ballparks that are being built are smaller than before because people seem to want to have the experience they have at Fenway. This is the last park of this size, with this kind of intimacy. It absolutely fits in with the arts and culture of Boston. It's one of the most identifiable parts of our town, and there are lots of great sports fans in music.

Fenway is totally iconic. When people say "Boston," "Fenway" is just about always the next thing that comes to mind. It's an institution just as Symphony Hall is a Boston institution. I think the ballpark itself is a national treasure, and now the surrounding area complements the ballpark.

The feeling here now is so much different than when I first came to Fenway. Obviously, these people really care about the overall feel of the ballpark. I know that there's real thought about how this space and the community connect. It's one of the few spaces where you gather people from every walk of life and every age group and they all share the experience. You can't say that about a lot of other things or other places.

In October of 2004 I was in Tokyo, doing the music on a mini-documentary. Now there are a lot of Yankees fans in Japan because of Hideki Matsui, but there was a large television in the lobby of the broadcast company, and they were broadcasting the moment that the Red Sox won the World Series.

After the Rolling Stones played here and they had some trouble with the field, Larry Lucchino said that next time they might just have me on the mound with my cello to save the field. I think he has a good sense of humor. If we did that, there would just be one small hole on the mound. I think the acoustics would be great. The only thing I might worry about are the echoes, but I know the organ sounds pretty good.

Jim Palmer

Jim Palmer was the only pitcher to win a World Series game in three different decades. He was inducted into the Hall of Fame in 1990.

I MET BILLY CRYSTAL IN THE EARLY '90S. *City Slickers* had come out, and when I saw him I reminded him of the great scene when they were all riding on the horses and they talked about your best day ever. In the movie, Billy talked about his dad taking him to Yankee Stadium and walking him through the tunnel and him seeing how green the grass was. Well, back in the late '70s, we [the Orioles] came to Boston on an off day, a Thursday. We were playing the Red Sox over the weekend. [Coach] Elrod Hendricks told me he'd meet me at Fenway around five o'clock to throw. So there I was, sitting in the outfield of an empty Fenway. There was not one person there. Not one. No guards. No Joe Mooney. I had come out early to do some running and I was sitting in the outfield, stretching. You could smell the ballpark. And there I am on the outfield grass and it's one of those 75-degree days with no humidity and a slight breeze and the sun is shining and the grass is glistening and I'm saying, "This is what it's all about."

The greatest day ever.

When I would come to Boston, I used to run up the ramp to see which way the wind was blowing to see if my neck would hurt from watching the home runs. Fenway is hitter friendly, obviously. It's a challenge to pitch in. It's about tradition. You think about all the great players that ever played there. I sit in Camden Yards, which is a wonderful place to play baseball, but it doesn't have the history. When we left Memorial Stadium, I said I just hoped the new place has as many good things happen as Memorial Stadium did.

Can you imagine taking a sleeping bag to Fenway Park and staying there at night and having the ghosts come and visit you? Just think of all the great players that played left field. And all the great games. That's what this game is all about. For me to have my whole career start there is really something.

My first game in the majors was at Fenway Park. I was nineteen. Robin Roberts was thirty-eight and he was my roommate. We were staying at the old Kenmore Hotel in Boston. I remember going out to dinner the night before and he picked up the check and I couldn't believe it. It was my first time in Boston and I loved it. Dave McNally and I hooked a ride on the MBTA because I'd always heard that song by the Kingston Trio—"Charlie on the MTA." I'd heard about the Wall, too. But I wasn't thinking about too many things. When you are nineteen, you're just happy to be there.

It was Opening Day in Boston and Robin started and we were ahead, 4–3, in the second inning and Hank Bauer called me in to face Tony Conigliaro with the bases loaded. I think it was snowing. I was nervous. When I got to the mound, Bauer asked me if I was nervous, and I said, "No, but what do I do with this extra ball?" I had carried the warm-up ball in from the bullpen. I threw Tony two high fastballs and he swung and missed both. Then I threw him a knee-high fastball and he took it and John Flaherty called it a strike. That was my introduction to Fenway Park. Later in the ball game, I threw a pitch up and away to Felix Mantilla, and he hit a pop fly down the left field line into the screen. The next time he came up, I accidentally threw a ball inside, and he swung so hard and splintered his bat so much they almost had to call the ground crew out to pick up the pieces of his bat. So I learned how to pitch in Fenway in my first game. It's funny, though. I never gave up a grand slam in 3,948 innings and could have given one up to the first batter I ever faced.

The fans in Boston are special. They want the Red Sox to win, but I think more than any town in baseball they respect the athletes that come in. Fans in Boston, because of the great job the newspapers did, and the closeness in the ballpark, it was like you were one of them. I always felt the fans there were really important, like a tenth man. It's the only place I ever pitched where the fans stood up on every fly ball because of the closeness of the fences. If you had a weak heart, you couldn't pitch there. You better get some runs and be on your game to win there. It's a park that tests you emotionally. Good pitchers a lot of times get hit. So it tests you physically and emotionally. You're going to experience some frustration. Our outfielders had trouble there. Don Buford had a ball go through his legs twice in left field. It skipped through once, then he turned around, and it came off the Wall back through his legs again.

The clubhouse was rough. When I first played, the only food they gave you was popcorn and Pepsi. Later, we got the leftover hamburgers from concessions. But it was Fenway Park. It was cramped, but you know what—when you're talking about clubhouse chemistry and being together, there's nothing like the locker room in Fenway Park. I think these clubhouses in the new parks today are too big, too sprawling. You don't even know who's getting dressed around you. You don't see your teammates.

At Fenway, you'd walk through the fans to get to the clubhouse, and when I go back now as a broadcaster it's like you're still playing. The people there just have tremendous respect for baseball, and I think the ballpark has a lot to do with it. Where else can you walk from your hotel downtown and get to where you're going to play?

Bud Selig

Bud Selig is the commissioner of baseball.

CLUBS GET TIRED OF ME TALKING ABOUT HISTORY all the time, but you can't really love baseball without loving history. There are only two parks that I've loved from the time I was a kid to now. One would be Wrigley Field in Chicago and the other would be Fenway Park in Boston. There is a uniqueness. Fenway and Wrigley manifest the history of the game better than any other ballparks I know. All you have to do is walk in and you feel it and sense it.

In 1949, my mother and I were in New York. I was a great Yankee fan, a great Joe DiMaggio fan. We went up to Boston, and my mother wanted to take me to art galleries and things like that. But she loved baseball and we went to Fenway Park. The Yankees were there. I was fifteen. We walked up to the ticket window. I'll never forget it. My mother told the man at the ticket window, "I've brought my boy from Milwaukee. We want to go to the game." He slammed the window and said, "Sorry, lady, we're sold out." My mother and I walked around Fenway for two hours trying to figure a way to get into the game. We never did. The first time I went to Fenway was about three or four years later, when I was still in college.

Of all the parks I enter, there are still two parks for sure that produce a feeling within me that brings back my youth. They look the same and feel the same, and that's Wrigley Field and Fenway Park. I think what they've done is remarkable. I'm delighted they are going to continue. And it is a testament to a history that should be kept as long as is humanly possible. Even with all the changes, it still looks like Fenway Park. There's going to be a question about how long they can stay there, but I certainly hope as long as I am commissioner and for years afterward. It is a remarkable franchise, given the support and the almost religious fervor, and that ballpark I believe is the center of it. It's a great thrill for me as commissioner to walk into a park like that, and it brings back memories of fifty-five to sixty years ago, and you want to preserve that. They've done a remarkable job of doing that.

Tim Russert

Tim Russert is the host of NBC's *Meet the Press* and the author of numerous best-selling books.

MY FIRST DAY AT FENWAY WAS IN 1970 OR 1971, when we made a road trip from John Carroll University in Cleveland to Boston. Outside the ballpark, I had an Italian sausage like I'd never had before. When the gates opened, I walked in, and all I can remember is green. Everything was green. I wanted to see the Monster right away, so I went as far as I could toward right field so I could look back over to left field and see the Monster.

It looked like a ballpark and felt like a ballpark. I had grown up in Buffalo, going to Offerman Stadium there. It was a small, compact park when compared with Cleveland, where I had gone to games in a place that sat 80,000. Every year for my birthday, my dad would load up the station wagon and we'd drive to Cleveland with my three uncles. I was the beer jockey in the back. We'd go to a Cleveland Indians doubleheader. Then suddenly, to see Fenway—it was a major league park that was small, compact, and green. You felt drawn to it. It just felt so natural being there. I felt like I was in a real ballpark. After that, every chance I had, I would work out my schedule, and if I had to be in Boston, the first thing I would check was the Red Sox schedule.

I returned to Fenway for a Red Sox game in 1993, the first time since my first visit. It was the first visit for my son, Luke, who was eight years old. He was born in New York City, and I had taken him to Yankee Stadium and Shea Stadium. And we had gone to spring training. And he'd been to Orioles games. But when we walked into Fenway, I told him, "This is a shrine." It turned out it was the day of Waco. My beeper went off, and we ran upstairs to a luxury box, and we were watching Waco and the burning fire and I had to leave the park. I had to go to the airport and fly home.

Probably the most magic night was the All-Star Game in 1999, and I brought Luke. Earlier in the day we had a chance to meet Ted Williams, and my son had a Yankees hat on and a T-shirt that said "Army." And

> All I can remember is green.
>
> Everything was green.
>
> — TIM RUSSERT

Williams said, "Kid, you got the wrong hat and the wrong shirt. I've only played for two teams my whole life and they're the two best teams ever, the Boston Red Sox and the Marine Corps." Then that night there was Ted on the golf cart with all the great players. By that time I was blessed and out of the bleachers, and we were right on top of it.

I had a chance to interview Pedro Martinez in the locker room at Fenway. He showed us all of the grips he used on the ball, and we talked a lot about him growing up in the Dominican Republic. Luke grew up with a Spanish nanny, so he was able to talk to Pedro in Spanish, and Pedro loved that. A couple of years later, I was also there on the Sunday night in 2004 when the Sox were playing the Yankees on the night before the Democratic National Convention started in Boston. I was sitting a few rows behind John Kerry, laughing at the whole scene.

When Luke was deciding on colleges, he chose Boston College, and I think Fenway had something to do with it. That was the fall of 2004, and I got a phone call one morning. It was Luke and he said, "Dad, you wouldn't believe it! I'm in the middle of a riot, but I'm okay." That was the night they won the World Series.

So that's what Fenway is about for me. So many memories going back to my time at college, and now my son is in college in Boston. Meeting Ted and Pedro. The biggest problem is that the beer lines are too long. I took my dad to Yankee Stadium and my dream is to bring him to Fenway. We'll get it done.

John Henry

John Henry is the owner of the Boston Red Sox.

I WAS NINE YEARS OLD WHEN I FIRST HAD THE opportunity to move beyond the days and nights of baseball on the radio and the occasional black-and-white telecast. One hallowed, sunny afternoon I was able to go to my first baseball game at a major league ballpark. The old Sportsman's Park in St. Louis was by far the most beautiful sight I had ever seen. It may have actually been a little run-down at that point, but to me it was beautiful beyond all description. I will never forget that first glimpse of the green playing field.

Forty years later I purchased the Florida Marlins, who were (and still are) badly in need of a new ballpark. While I was in the process of trying to get a new ballpark for them, I traveled to virtually every major league ball-park in America to study each of their strengths and weaknesses. I was wowed by the new parks in Baltimore, Denver, Houston, Atlanta, and Phoenix. Meanwhile, San Francisco, Detroit, San Diego, and Pittsburgh were build-ing new parks. In each one, the owners would mention

what their new parks had in common with either Wrigley Field or Fenway Park. Sometimes both. It seemed that everyone wanted to borrow some of the nostalgia of the ancient ballyards. The Florida Marlins had a Teal Monster, and Camden Yards had its version of Yawkey Way on Eutaw Street. As the new parks were built, they got smaller and asymmetrical.

Buying the Red Sox in 2002 was the realization of a lifetime dream, and I was at once honored and awed to have an office in Fenway Park. The draw to Fenway was strong. I literally could not drive past the ballpark without going inside. Often I would go there just to walk, to drink in the solace and peace of an empty Fenway when the Red Sox were out of season or on the road.

Fenway speaks to all of us in New England, and we all hear different things. To me she whispers stories of the past—players and events of decades gone by—and there is great satisfaction in her voice. She's seen it all, and much of what she has witnessed involves things that did not happen on the playing field. The ballpark and its lore connect generations of families across New England and throughout the world. And those memories, ones I still cherish from my earliest days as a baseball fan, continue to inspire my imagination and enrich my life. Being in Fenway or just thinking about it reminds me that there is going to be another ball game played soon.

My favorite baseball photographs are some of the shots that fill earlier pages of this book, images captured by Stan Grossfeld. The framed photos hang on the walls of our box behind home plate, and I think of them as Norman Rockwells for a new generation. I still see those faces at Fenway every time we play a home game. Families these days often can't find time or manage schedules that will allow for three solid hours of family conversation, but it still happens when they come to the ballpark—and that, too, is part of the magic of Fenway.

Senator Edward M. Kennedy

A lifelong public servant, Edward M. Kennedy has represented Massachusetts in the United States Senate since 1962.

I HAVE A LOT OF MEMORIES ABOUT FENWAY. IT really goes back to both of my grandfathers, Patrick Kennedy and Honey Fitz. I grew up very close to Honey Fitz. My father was in England during the war, and when we came back here I was sent off to boarding school when I was about seven or eight years old. And I went in every Sunday to see my grandfather Honey Fitz. He was really a surrogate father to me. And he was the one that brought me to Fenway Park. This was around 1943, 1944. Grandpa, of course, was a member of the Royal Rooters and a hardcore Red Sox fanatic. I remember him showing me that picture of him throwing out the ball—the first ball at Fenway in April of 1912 and in the World Series again that fall. I can still see him leading the Red Sox in the parade in Boston when they won the World Series. My mother had it up at the house until recent years. She is the one directly to his left, and the other woman is Agnes, my mother's sister.

My father was captain of the baseball team at Boston Latin and also played baseball at Harvard. He loved the game. I think that all of us, growing up, were a little wary. We knew that Dad had played and played well.

I went to Fenway with my brothers, Jack and Bobby, and I went with my father. The last time I remember was in 1967, when we had those last two days of the regular season against the Twins and my brother Bob and I took my dad. He had been ill for some time. Senator Humphrey was at one of those games, and it was great fun ribbing him about who was going to win. The Red Sox finally won (6–4) and clinched the pennant the next day. Jose Santiago was the pitcher that day and he gave me the winning ball, which I still have on display in my Boston office. And I've got Carl Yastrzemski's 1967 MVP Award, and he gave me the Gold Glove.

I think the 2004 Red Sox comeback against the Yankees was probably the greatest athletic sequence of events in the history of sports. I was not there that often because I was around the campaign a lot. I think probably my favorite moment of being in Fenway Park would be the sixth game of the 1975 World Series, when Carlton Fisk hit the home run against the Reds. No true Red Sox fan can forget that game. I still remember Bernie Carbo hitting the pinch-hit home run to tie the game, and then Fisk, after midnight, in the bottom of the twelfth inning. We unfortunately failed to win the World Series, but I think that is probably the greatest moment.

My grandfather took me to my first game probably when I was seven years old. The thing I always thought about Fenway Park was that it's the best ballpark in America with the most rabid fans. It's got a tradition and a history. In a world where there's such transition and movement of people—they say a quarter of our country moves every two years—but most people at Fenway Park saw their first game with their father or their grandfather right there in Fenway Park. There's an indelible tradition that runs through that. It's part of the lore. It's the loyalty to the Red Sox. People know that things happened there, and it's so much a part of Boston. I think that's an intangible ingredient that's unique and special. You can go to other games in other ballparks, but this is it.

The Red Sox called me about throwing out the first ball in 2012, when Fenway Park celebrates its 100th birthday. I'm practicing. I've been watching and checking the distance and getting ready. That would be great, especially since Grandpa threw the ball out in 1912.

Last year one of the nice events was when the National Historic Association gave the presentation to the Red Sox to preserve Fenway Park. It's recognized as a historic site. The new Red Sox owners could have done a lot of different things, but they understood the importance of Fenway Park to the fans and to the people, and I think everybody is thrilled with that.

Bucky Dent

Bucky Dent hit forty homers in eleven big league seasons, including a Fenway fly ball that won the 1978 Yankees–Red Sox playoff game.

I WAS WITH THE WHITE SOX THE FIRST TIME I CAME to Fenway. Everybody had always talked about it. It's kind of like Yankee Stadium and Wrigley Field. You hear a lot about it, but when you actually walk out there and see the Wall, you realize what an impact it has on you as a player. It's a neat place. It was always a fun place to play, but as a visitor, it was always a scary place to play. A lead is never safe. I remember being up by six runs late in a game with the White Sox and we

lost. You never knew what was going to happen. It was the same thing when I was with the Cardinals, playing at Wrigley Field.

I hit the Wall a few times and hit a few home runs here. As a shortstop, it presented some unique situations. When I first came here, they made sure I knew that when a ball went down the line I had to come out, because it might come off that wall and kick back toward the infield.

When I went to bat in the playoff game, I was just trying to get a base hit. We were down two runs. I never thought about trying to hit a home run, it's just that here, if you get a ball inside, it's possible to hit a home run, to be able to jerk one out. In that situation, I got a pitch that I could pull, and I happened to hit it on a line. When I hit the ball, I didn't think it was going out. I didn't think it was high enough to get over the Wall. I thought it was going to hit the top of the Wall. When I hit it, I was trying to run from home plate to get to second. When I was rounding first, I saw the signal that it went out. I never saw it go over the Wall.

It's always special for me to come back here. It's just a good place to come and play. The crowd is on you, and you've got the Wall in left field, and the game is different every time. It's a lot of fun. I coached first

Bucky Dent is congratulated by Roy White (6) after hitting his homer during a playoff game at Fenway in 1978.

base here one night with Texas, and they booed me.

It's always going to be there. I come to Boston a lot because I do some PR for a company in Auburn, Massachusetts. It's unbelievable. I met the guy that owns the company at a Yankee Fantasy Camp. We hit it off, and here I am twelve years later. I go back and forth every year to Boston. I come up to play golf or talk baseball with the customers. I enjoy it. It's fun to come back here. It's interesting because everybody knows where they were when I hit the home run. It's something because of the magnitude of the Red Sox history and the Yankee history, our catching them on the last day. There was so much riding on that game. It was a special day. One of those things that doesn't come along very often.

When I travel around in the Boston area, there isn't a day that goes by when I don't have somebody come up to me and tell me I broke their heart thirty years ago. Everybody kind of remembers that game and that day. I remember a couple of years ago I came up here to play some golf with some customers on Cape Cod. There was a bar out there and the bartender was a diehard Red Sox fan, and after the golf game they told me, "You've got to come over and see this guy. We're going to bring you in there, sit you down, and see if this guy recognizes you." It was the year of the strike, and he was such a big fan, he had all the baseball hats in his bar covered up because of the strike. So I walked in and sat down, and he looked at me and his face kind of dropped. I said, "Hi, I'm Bucky Dent," and he said, "I know who you are." It happens.

When people tell me they are Red Sox fans, I like to joke around with them and get them talking about that season. I remember that last at-bat of that playoff game. I remember standing at shortstop for the matchup between Gossage and Yastrzemski. I can still see Gossage throwing a fastball right down the middle that popped him up. Those things just don't go away.

We have Little Fenway at my baseball school in Delray Beach, Florida. We were going to redo one field and we just felt it would be neat to do something different for the kids. A lot of the kids will never experience playing in Fenway, so putting up a normal field

was nothing new. We wanted to give them a feel of playing in a ballpark with that kind of atmosphere, or a visualization of hitting one out. That's what we created. And over the years, the dads have really gotten a charge out of going out there and trying to hit one out. We tried to build it the same. The only difference is that this wall is 37 feet and ours is 34.

I'd hate to see them tear down Fenway. It's like Yankee Stadium. There's just certain parks that have that magical feeling when you walk in 'em. The new stadiums are nice, but there's just something magical about Yankee Stadium, Wrigley Field, and Fenway. They're special places, but you don't have that atmosphere anymore. I'd find a way to redo the stadium and keep that mystique of what it's all about.

When you're talking about Fenway, you're talking about The Game. The one game for me.

The big thing about Fenway is the crowd.

When you come out of that bullpen

    it's kind of weird.

It's like in the days of the Romans

    in the Colosseum.

— DENNIS ECKERSLEY

Dennis Eckersley

Dennis Eckersley pitched in the major leagues from 1975 to 1998. He was inducted into the Hall of Fame in 2004.

TO ME, FENWAY IS WHERE I LEARNED WHAT baseball is all about. What did I know? I'd been in Cleveland. If you're just talking about pitching, Fenway's not good. I've seen a lot of things happen there that wouldn't happen anywhere else. They say left-handers can't pitch there, but that's not true. But if you pitch there long enough, it's going to take its toll. There's no foul territory. I'm a flyball pitcher, and sometimes you can't overcome that. It could come at a key point. You got two outs and there's a pop-up that would have been caught anywhere else, but it's in the stands at Fenway, and then the next pitch is a double. It can be devastating. I think you have to be a power pitcher to pitch there for a long time. You cannot be a finesse pitcher. Put Greg Maddux in this son-of-a-bitch and let's see what he can do. As great as he is, he would not be as good as he is now.

More than anything, I think left-handed hitters can do well there, especially if they can stay behind the ball like Yaz did and Fred Lynn and Mo Vaughn. Left-handed hitters are tougher than right-handers. They take away the outside part of the plate, so you pitch them in and make them pull the ball. But nobody pulls the ball anymore. I got away with it. The first year I was there [1978], I was 11–1. I don't know why. I said I was letting left-handers pull the ball, but I didn't know. I was lucky.

The big thing about Fenway is the crowd. That's how it begins when you are a starting pitcher. It's especially true the first time you go there as a visiting pitcher and warm up in the bullpen. When you come out of that bullpen it's kind of weird. It's like in the days of the Romans in the Colosseum. When you're going good, they sort of cheer as you're coming out of that gate. If you're not going too well, they hoot on you.

The bullpen crowd was crazier thirty years ago. Years ago, I could smell weed out there. And it's loud, even though it's wide open. It can be intimidating for an opposing player, and it can help the home team. People don't realize that it's not like that in all ballparks. In Oakland the crowds didn't mean anything. Fenway is loud. Maybe it's because they're right on you. The only place you can hide is right field. Everyplace else, they're right on you. There's no other park like that.

I like driving to Fenway now. When I first came, I was intimidated by the aggressive people. It was scary. Fenway is the most cramped. Like our player parking lot. You don't bring your nice car, 'cuz it'll get wailed.

Don Zimmer

Don Zimmer was manager of the Red Sox for five seasons and has been in professional baseball for six decades.

I'VE BEEN IN BASEBALL FOR ALMOST SIXTY YEARS, and the first time I saw Fenway was when I made the All-Star team in 1961. Danny Murtaugh chose me as an extra man. All second basemen that year were having bad years. That was one of the years they had two All-Star games, one in San Francisco and one in Boston. I walked into Fenway for the first time, and being a right-handed hitter, it looked very inviting.

Fenway has always been a special place for me. People have asked me in the last ten or fifteen years about my favorite parks, and I've always said one was Fenway and the other was Wrigley Field. When I stop

and look back, I always say I'm a lucky man. Baseball was something I wanted to do all my life, and I got to manage at both Fenway and Wrigley Field.

There's a difference when you manage in those parks. Fenway and Wrigley are two of the toughest parks to manage in. In Fenway, it's the left field fence. You manage differently. When the wind is blowing out, why give up an out in a bunt situation? You know the score is gonna wind up 10–8 or 13–12. In Boston I ran less because I had a good offensive lineup. There were some left-handed pitchers that had great success there. Bill Lee won 17 games three straight years. Roger Moret. I was never scared of pitching a left-hander in Fenway.

You really get an education coaching third base in Fenway Park. Without a doubt, it's the toughest park in America to coach third in. First of all, you got men on base and they are running, and a guy hits a ball over the third base bag and you're ready to send two or three guys home, and the ball hits that wall that sticks out and bounces out to shortstop . . . or it gets by the Wall and gets all the way down in the corner, and you almost have to go out on the playing field to see where the ball is. I probably went into fair territory a few times to see what was going on.

I coached third there for parts of three seasons. We had a good club and the fans were great fans. They were close. No question about it. In the sixth game of the World Series in 1975, Pete Rose was playing third base, and we had the bases loaded and nobody out and I had told our runner on third, Denny Doyle, that anything that looks like a line drive, get back to the base. The next ball was hit up high to left and I told him to tag up. When I realized it wasn't far enough to take a chance, I ran back to third base and said, "Don't go anywhere." Then I saw him take off and I thought he was faking. I hollered, "No, no, no!" He came up with a story that he thought I said, "Go, go, go!" Ask Pete Rose. He heard me. If we had lost that game, I had planned to leave early so that Denny wouldn't be put on the spot. Fortunately, we won the game. I remember twice during that game Pete told me, "Win or lose, this might be the greatest game I've ever played in."

They all talk about Fenway Park being a hitter's park, but whenever there's an advantage, somewhere along the line there's a disadvantage. A lot of guys hit a line drive that would be a home run anywhere in baseball and it goes for a single in Fenway, off the Wall. Then you hit a high fly ball that's in the net. Here's an advantage for a pitcher. You're winning, 2–1, in the eighth inning. You strike out the first two hitters and the next guy hits a double. Then the next guy singles to left and the third base coach can't send him home. So because you're in Fenway, you get another chance to get out of the inning.

In '78 we had that big lead and we stopped hitting. The Yankees caught us and went ahead of us. People said we choked and were gone, and for a time it looked like we were. Then we won our last 8 games and tied them. When I went to the park Monday morning, at around 7:30 A.M. for that playoff game, it was about the biggest thrill I'd ever had. Just thinking of getting into that park and playing that game. And probably the biggest disappointment I've ever had was losing that game. It looked like we had the game won two or three times. Unfortunately, we didn't win. Lou Piniella caught that ball in the sun in right field (Jerry Remy's one-hop single in the ninth), and to this day he doesn't know how he caught the ball.

The Dent homer I remember like it was yesterday. Usually in October at Fenway the wind would be blowing in. It would be cool. On that day it was warm and the wind was drifting out a little. When you're in that park every day for five years like I was, usually you know where the ball is going when it's hit. When Dent hit that ball, I said, "Good, that's an out." Then I saw Yaz going back, and when he turned around, I said, "Well, that ain't so bad, it's off the Wall." Then the ball went in the net.

That was something. We won 99 games and got to the playoff game. The next year we open at home with Cleveland, and I take out the lineup card and Dave Garcia's there for the Indians. When I walk out of the dugout I got booed by thirty thousand people. Garcia looked at me and said, "I don't think I could take it here. I really feel bad for you."

You got to do something awful bad to get booed in Chicago. Fenway's different. I learned to live with the fans. I really believe that Bill Lee started most of that. He'd go to the media. He made up names for me. He went to the bullpen and had all those hoodlums out there. I think that rubbed off on some of the fans and they started booing, and it became somewhat of a ritual. I learned to live with it. I can remember one night when my daughter came to the game with my wife. My daughter was a grown woman by then. We were driving home on Route 93 over the bridge and I heard my daughter sniffling. I said, "What the hell is going on?" I looked in the back seat and she was crying like a baby. She said, "Daddy, I'm so tired of you getting booed." I told her to stay home if that was going to bother her.

At Fenway, the fans in the cheap seats would come from way up high, down by the dugout to get me. I never fought with 'em. They'd call me a bum, and every now and then I'd look up at them and say, "You know something, you may be right." I worked in Fenway for seven years. In almost sixty years of baseball, that's the longest I spent in any place.

James Earl Jones

James Earl Jones appeared in the 1989 film *Field of Dreams*.

I GREW UP IN MICHIGAN. AT THAT TIME BASEBALL was still segregated, so I didn't really go to see baseball. We had traveling teams in our county and I'd go to those games, but not the major leagues. I was never a major league baseball fan.

I came to Fenway Park in association with *Field of Dreams*. It didn't make me a baseball fan, but it made me understand and appreciate the game. I had not been to Fenway before. I had heard about it from [the film critic] Jeffrey Lyons, who is a staunch Red Sox fan. He can't say enough about Fenway.

When you walk into that stadium, you fall in love with the grass. You fall in love with that field of dreams and the design, and I think every stadium in the country should have some of that. It's a wonderful place. I also noticed how close it is to the city and the nature of the fans.

We didn't go on the field. We just stayed in the stands. We were only there one day. We had a small group of extras who sat behind us and in front in our section. Most of the time, Kevin Costner and I were relating to the scoreboard. He'd say, "Did you see that?" and I'd say, "What?" There was no ball game at the time we were shooting. You cannot ask professional players to keep repeating the way actors do.

The movie was definitely about baseball and about fathers and sons. Bart Giamatti's books have the same kind of poetry as Kinsella's. I don't know if they ever knew each other. My wife always read scripts, and she read that script and said, "They will leave the baseball speech on the cutting room floor, but you've got to do this movie."

I'm most proud of the work I've done that draws from small projects. By that I mean simple stories. And *Field of Dreams* qualifies as a small story and also a successful film. In that movie, we were talking about spirit and magic, and to cover that, Fenway was the ideal park.

Field of Dreams qualifies as

a small story and also a successful film.

In that movie, we were talking about

spirit and magic, and to cover that,

Fenway was the ideal park.

— JAMES EARL JONES

Carl Yastrzemski

Carl Yastrzemski played for the Red Sox from 1961 to 1983 and was inducted into the Hall of Fame in 1989.

I FIRST VISITED FENWAY IN 1959 WHEN I SIGNED. We went around to all the different teams I was interested in signing with. I did a Thanksgiving vacation tour my freshman year at Notre Dame when I made up my mind to sign. I stopped at Cincinnati first, then Detroit, then Fenway. Cincinnati had Crosley Field, which was a great ballpark to hit in, and Detroit's a great ballpark to hit in. I walked into Fenway and it was snowing. And I'm standing up by the executive offices overlooking the field with my dad. Somebody said, "Boy, this is a good ballpark to hit in," and I looked and said, "Jesus Christ, you can't even see right field, it's so far away." And after coming from Detroit and Crosley Field, it did look far. To tell you the truth, I was more interested in going either with the Yankees or Cincinnati or Detroit because of the ballparks. But my dad had a priest friend on Long Island, Father Joe. And he kept saying, "You have to play for Mr. Yawkey." At that time, my dad had to cosign the contract, so that's how I ended up with the Red Sox.

I think Fenway's a great ballpark for the fans. The new one, they keep talking about it, but I don't see anything happening. So I don't even worry about it. I think Fenway's great and they should keep it, but maybe for financial reasons they have to come up with a new ballpark. I like these new ballparks in Cleveland and Baltimore. They're good hitters' ballparks and you got a lot of action and the fans are close. I hated those symmetrical ballparks.

I think the closeness of the seats in Fenway is what I liked the best. You'd come off a road trip where you played in Cleveland or Oakland, like you were in some coliseum where the fans weren't into it and it was hard for you to get into it. But as soon as you stepped onto the field at Fenway Park, you got into it real quick because of the closeness of those seats.

I've always said, you can't hide in it. If you have a horseshit day, everybody sees it at the ballpark and writes about it in the papers. People see it on TV. Why cover it up? Just admit to it. It's that simple. You're human. I inter-acted with the fans a little bit between innings. I think by doing it, you would win 'em over on your side, instead of ignoring them. The scoreboard guys kept me informed. They had a couple of kids out there. Joe Mooney's ground crew. Joe would throw them in there as punishment, I think.

When I first got to Boston, the Wall was cement and then tin. Then they went with the plastic or whatever they call it now. When they put that in, back in the late '70s, it was easier to play the Wall. Before, when you had the tin and the rivets, and those two-by-fours every few feet, you never knew where the ball was going to come off. If it hit the two-by-fours, the ball would bounce back just as if it had hit the cement. If it hit the dead spot, it would just drop down. Then it might rattle around the ladder and you'd just have to wait for it to come down. There was nothing you could do. It made it interesting playing there. But I loved having that thing behind me. I can remember Frank Howard coming into Fenway Park and I'd play him right behind shortstop. And I'd play between short and third base, trying to take away the line drive base hit. Or make a play on him at first base. Playing left field at Fenway, you took a position where you don't have so much action and made it into a place where you had a lot of action. Decoying. Stuff like that. The pitchers used to get pissed off if I didn't move on a home run. They'd say, "Jesus Christ, at least make an attempt to go back." But I was setting it up for a case when if a guy hit a ball that I knew was going to go off the Wall, I'd stand there like I knew it was going to be a home run, and maybe he'd start trotting to first and we could hold him to a single. So there was a method to doing all that. When they take the Wall down and move into a new park, I want to get a little piece of it.

I loved Fenway. I just loved it there. I knew everybody by their name. I knew all the concessions people, and I'd stop in there before the games. When you came to the ballpark, to me it was like being at home. It was like just going to your home.

You get the truth out of everyone

when you take them to Fenway.

— MIKE BARNICLE

I loved Fenway.

When you came to the ballpark,

to me it was like being at home.

It was like just going to your home.

— **CARL YASTRZEMSKI**

acknowledgments   The authors would like to thank Lee Serra, Judy Bailey, Dick Johnson, Kevin Shea, Kate Gordon, Tim Samway, Dan Casey, Matt Storin, Ben Taylor, Ben Bradlee Jr., Don Skwar, Kate Shaughnessy, Stephen Stills, Steve Sheppard, Robin Young, Renee Masi, Lesley Visser, Meg Blackstone, Mike Barnicle, Ed Kleven, Kevin Dupont, Peter Gammons, Dave Smith, Bill Tanton, Vince Doria, Tim Kurkjian, Laurel Prieb, Wendy Selig-Prieb, Phyllis Merhige, Joe Sullivan, Guy Spina, Bob Lobel, Bob Levin, John Iannacci, John Horn, Eric Monroe, Dick Bresciani, John Henry, Tom Werner, Larry Lucchino, Dr. Charles Steinberg, John Blake, Peter Chase, Pam Ganley, Colleen Reilly, Andrew Merle, Jonathan Stone, Mary Jane Ryan, Kathleen Cable, Debbie Matson, Tom Mulvoy, Sean Mullin, Jonny Miller, Mike McHugh, Gordon Edes, Jeff Idelson, Sue Callaghan, and all those who agreed to be interviewed.

Thanks to the Hood blimp, Paul Comerford, Bruce Springsteen, Mayor Thomas Menino, Lynne Smith, Deborah Wrobleski, Steve Shaughnessy, Shaughnessy Aerialifts, Jim Davis, Brian Kaplan, Dr. Elisa Fulton, Mary Beth Kabat, Jean Shiner, Erica Pearl, Samantha Palmer, Peter Southwick, the *Globe*'s Photo Department, Vincent Musi, Callie Shell, Wil Haygood, Tim Dwyer, Julia Talcott, Mike LaVigne, Michael Sturgis, Catie Aldrich, Nikon Professional Services, Zona Color Lab in Cambridge, and the New England Sports Museum.

Special thanks to Gary Smith for believing in the project and to Susan Canavan, Melissa Lotfy, Will Vincent, Megan Wilson, and Luise Erdmann at Houghton Mifflin. And to Joe Mooney. Thanks to Bill Marr and Sarah Leen, Legal Sea Foods, Arthur D'Angelo of Twins Enterprises, and Sue Stevens, Dave Walsh, and the staff at Skipjack's.

As always, a big thanks to our families. Dan appreciates the help and patience of Marilou, Sarah, Kate, and Sam. Stan would like to thank his wife, Stacey Kabat, for being a temporary baseball widow, his son Samuel, his dad Purroy, his mother Mildred, his sister Sandy, and Howie and Bert Bauer, who got him tickets to the 1967 World Series.